ABSTRACTS
OF
Bledsoe County
Tennessee

COUNTY COURT MINUTES

1841–1846

WPA RECORDS

Heritage Books
2024

HERITAGE BOOKS

AN IMPRINT OF HERITAGE BOOKS, INC.

Books, CDs, and more—Worldwide

For our listing of thousands of titles see our website
at
www.HeritageBooks.com

A Facsimile Reprint
Published 2024 by
HERITAGE BOOKS, INC.
Publishing Division
5810 Ruatan Street
Berwyn Heights, MD 20740

International Standard Book Number
Paperbound: 978-0-7884-8960-0

IN THE 1930s THE WPA HAD WORKERS TO COPY RECORDS IN THE COUNTY
COURTHOUSE. THIS VOLUME IS AN ABSTRACT FROM A MICROFILM COPY.
WE REALIZE SOME OF THE NAMES ARE NOT SPELLED CORRECTLY. HOWEVER,
IT MAY BE THE EXACT TRANSCRIPTION OF THE CLERK'S ENTRY. MANY
WORDS ARE MISSPELLED, BUT THIS MAY ALODS BE THE WAY IT IS ENTERED
IN THE MINUTE BOOK. IN MANY CASES, THE CLERK DID NOT USE
PUNCTUATION, AND THE MEANING OF THE ENTRY IS NOT TOO CLEAR. THE
ORIGINAL BOOK MAY BE SEEN IN THE OFFICE OF THE COUNTY CLERK,
BLEDSOE COUNTY, TENNESSEE

COUNTY COURT MINUTES
(ABSTRACT)

1841-1846

BLEDSOE COUNTY
TENNESSEE

BLEDSOE COUNTY, TENNESSEE

COUNTY COURT MINUTE BOOK
VOLUME 1
1841-1846

September Session 1841

P. 1   Present on the bench: John M. BEATTY, William BROWN,
        and Aron SCHOOLFIELD, Esqrs.

        James SPARKS tendered his resignation as constable in
        the 6th district...received by the court.

        James A. TULLOSS, Clerk of court, presented a settlement
        made with Mary MASSY, Guardian of the minor heirs of
        Richard MASSY, Deceased...ordered to be spread on record.

        James A. TULLOSS, clerk, presented a settlement made with
        William FOSTER, guardian of the minor heirs of David
        POINER, deceased...ordered to be spread on record.

        James ALLEN, guardian of minor heirs of Thomas INGRAM,
        deceased, tendered his resignation as such guardian.to
        Hester A. INGRAM and James E. INGRAM...received.

P. 3   Ephriam NELSON produced certificate from Bird THOMAS
        certifying that he had been elected constable for the
        9th district...took oath to support Constitutionof U.S.
        and State of Tenn., and an oath against duelling, and
        oath of office...entered into bond.   A. H. COULTER and
        Joseph HIXSON, securities...bond, $4,000.00

        George REAL, guardian to minor heirs of William GREEN,
        deceased, resigned his guardianship...accepted by court.

        James A. TULLOSS, Clerk, presented settlement made with
        Joseph HIXSON, guardian to minor heirs of John HIXSON,
        deceased...inspected, ordered to be spread on record

        Court appropriated the sum of $12.50 for support of
        Sarah KEENER, an old and infirm woman, for nest 6 months
        ...to be placed in hands of John M. BEATTY, who shall
        make report.

P. 4   Isaac ROBERSON appointed guardian to the minor heirs of
        William GREER?, deceased...entered into bond.

October Session 1841

        Present on the bench: John M. BEATTY, Aron SCHOOLFIELD,
        William STEPHENS, Burell LEE, William BROWN, William
        FOSTER, Isaac ROBERSON, Thomas J. RODGERS, Joseph
        HIXSON, and Peter D. WILLCOX.

P. 5   James A. TULLOSS, Clerk of this Court, presented receipt
        from the Comptroller of Tennessee for revenue collected
        from 1 Sept. 1840 to 1 Sept 1841... $381.83, less
        commission...$367.29.

        William WALKER's receipt as Trustee of Bledsoe County
        Received of James A. TULLOSS...$68.61 for same period.

P. 6   William WALKER's receipt for $49.68 from TULLOSS...
        money collected by him from merchants on Court house
        Tax for year 1841

        Burell LEE, John M. BEATTY, Ruben BROWN, Martin A. SMITH,
        and Isaac ANDERSON appointed jury of view on the public
        road passing by Samuel BILLINGSLEYs to Pikeville,
        commencing near the Top of the Hill toward Pikeville...
        to make report next term.

        John KIMMER released from paying half praised value of
        two stray horses-posted by him on 19 October 1839.

        William HICKSON released from the half praised value one
        stray steer, posted by him 12 Dec 1839.

        Ordered that a certificate issue to A. H. COULTER,
        cornor of Bledsoe County, "for summoning a juryof Enquest
        on the Body of a Deceased Child found in Sequatchie River
        ...$5.00

P. 7   James A. TULLOSS allowed $4.00 for a Record Book by him
        furnished

        Jesee BROWN appointed Overseer in room and stead of James
        STEPHENS, with the following hands and bound...
        Commencing at old John PARHAMs thence to John PRESTLEYS
        on the mountain to enclude Point BARGERS? and William
        PRESTLEYS to James HOUSTONS then to Obidiah WRIGHTS on a
        straight line to Sequatchie River thence to TOLLETT Mill
        to Enclude the hand to TOLLETTs store thence to Joseph
        PATTONs and John PARHAMs to the Beginning.

        Ordered that James SWAFFORD be appointed Overseer of
        the public road, second class, in room and stead of
        Real H. MILLARD, with same hands and bounds.

        John SMITH, Overseer on the Stage Road from Standifers
        Still house branch to the County line...Encluding hands
        thereon as follows: James THOMPSON, John TEATERS, A. B.
        EWTON, Philip HOOTS, Elijah AUSTON, James CLEMONS(?),
        George JONES, Thomas MATTHEWS, Jacob NEWMAN, Thomas A.
        POPE, James G. POPE, Linzy HOOTS, Frederick HOPKINS,
        Ezikiel MCVAY, John HOOTS, Edward SPARKMAN and Young
        EPERSON

Robert DREGGIN allowed $1.00 fro serving as constable one day at November Term 1840.

William WORTHINGTON allowed sum of $5.00 for attending as juror at July Term 1841

Jury of View: William BROWN, John M. BEATTY, James L. SCHOOLFIELD, Burell LEE and Bird THOMAS...on the Valley Road near said Wetherstons thence up Cumberland Mountain, the distance of ¼ mile, for the purpose of changing road.

Matthew PENDERGRASS and James CANTRELL allowed sum of $2.00 for Burial Expenses for a Deceased child found in Sequatchie River.

p. 9 Bond of James P. SPRING who was appointed guardian of Philander D. MOORE, a minor orphan (male)...security: Aron SCHOOLFIELD, John BRIDGMAN...$100.00

Following allowed sum of $2.00 fro attending as jurors in the trial of the state against William GOFF, for passing counterfeit money: Henry DUGER, William R. COOK, William HALE, Jeremiah CLOUD, Abel HARRISON, George H. BILLINGSLEY, Eli TURNER, William JONES, Nicholad NANEY, Enoc GREEN, Thomas MOONYHAM, Jr., Barnibus THOMAS.

William G. DALTON, jailor of Bledsoe County, allowed $33.75 , in the following cases: The state vs. Solomon GODSEY, $7.75; the state vs David REED, $15.50; the state vs Herman EDWARD, $5.00

Ordered that J. N. LOVE have the use of one of the jury rooms below stairs to work in as a Taylor, provided he keep the said house clean, doors shut, hoggs kept out, and to surrender the same at the Circuit Court.

p. 11 Ordered that Thomas FOSTER, Deputie Shreiff of this county be released from the poll Tax on the following pursons to wit, for the year 1841: Isaac M. SEAG?, Richard M. CATCHUM, Joseph PEW, Sam C. WORLEY, Henry KINZY, William DUSSEE?, Nathan HOWARD, Andrew HOLDER, Harry H. HOLLAND, Joseph B. LEATHERS?, James PICKETT, William B. SNOTGRASS, Young EPERSON, Daniel HORN, Isaac MILLER, George W. COLEMAN, William DOTSON, Joel DOTSON, Tilman, HANEY, John T. FLEMAN, J. A. JAMES, Benjamin LOONY, Joseph MCCLINE, Thomas MANSFIELD, Fielding TURNER, William WELCH, Marydeth WELCH, Bird SMITH, Leny? SMITH, and Joseph SMITH.

Ordered that John WILLSON be released from paying a poll tax for year 1841.

Bond of John M. BEATTY, Chairman of the County Court... $2,000.00..securities: W. Bird THOMAS, William

STEPHENS, J. BRIDGMAN.

P. 12   Sum of $10.00 appropriated to repair the Bridge near
         Barny THOMAS and Isaac ROBERSON and William WALKER to
         superintend the said repairs

         Ordered that the Collector of the Court house Tax pay
         over the amount by him collected to Thomas CRUTCHFIELD.

P. 13   William STEPHENS, Esqr tendered his resignation as
         Justice of the peace for Bledsoe County...accepted

November Session 1841

         Present on the bench: Isaac ROBERSON, William BROWN
         and Thomas J. ROGERS Esqr.

         James A. TULLOSS produced settlement made with Robert
         OWENS, administrator of estate of William GREER,
         deceased...inspected, ordered to be spread on record

p. 14   James A. TULLOSS produced settlement made with William
         KEARLY, guardian of minor heirs of Daniel KERLY...
         inspected, ordered to be spread on record

         James T. NANNY presented certificate from Bird THOMAS,
         sheriff, stateing he had been duly elected a constable
         in 6th district...entered into bond...took oaths

         Bond of James T. NANNY...$4,000.00...securities,
          John BRIDGMAN, M. A. SMITH

p. 16   December Session 1841

         On the bench: John M. BEATTY, Burrell LEA, Aron
         SCHOOLFIELD, Isaac ROBERSON Esqr.

         Ordered that the following named gentleman be appointed
         Revinew Commissioners to take in a list of the taxable
         property and polls...for the year 1842:
                        1st District..Peter D. WILCOX
                   2   "   Wiley REDWINE
                   3   "   Burrell LEA
                   4   "   William BROWN
                   5   "   John BILLINGSLEY
                   6   "   Saml. W. ROBERSON
                   7   "   Aron SCHOOLFIELD
                   8   "   Isaac ROBERSON
                   9   "   Joseph HIXSON
                                     Alexander LAMB
                   10   "   Joel WHEELER

p. 17   On application of James A. TULLOSS, he is appointed
         administrator of estate of William HENSON, deceased...
         entered into bond.. Letters of Administration issued

On application of Susan SMITH, widow and relict of
David SMITH, deceased, Byram HEARD appointed administrator
...entered into bond

On application of Susan SMITH, widow and relict of David
SMITH, deceased...departed this life intestate... court
appoints Jonathan POPE, Jacob NEWMAN and Robert OWENS to
set apart so much of the crop, stock and provisions and
monies on hand for support of said widow and her family/

p. 18 Sheriff to summons the following to attend the circuit
court as Jurors at next March term: George DAWSON, Jas.
M. REVIS, Wiley REDWINE, James WALKER, Senr., S. C. LOWE,
Burrell LEA, Aron SCHOOLFIELD, J. M. BEATTY, Alfred
SWAFFORD, Joseph MCDOWELL, William L. BROWN, M. A. SMITH,
John T. SWAFFORD, Peter HOODENPYLE, John SKILLERN, Elisha
KIRKLIN, Lewis KEEDY, Jr., Aron SWAFFORD, Thomas FOSTER,
Isaac ROBERSON, Buckner HOWARD, Alexander LAMB, Joseph
HIXSON, Joel WHEELER, Byram HEARD, and that Milcom
OWENS and David D. CARDER constables, wait on court.

This day Robert A. RENFRO tendered his resignation as
Constable/...accepted

P. 19 Ordered that Sheriff bring to the next term of court,
Nancy NEWBY, an insane woman, for the purpose of letting
her out to the lowest bidder.

Thomas FOSTER produced a receipt...received of Craven
SHERILL...taxes for the year 1841...$119.36, being the
amount of the poor house tax..s/James LOYD, Treasurer
of the poor house

On application of Widow INGRAM, Robert OWENS appointed
guardian of the minor heirs of Thomas INGRAM, deceased

Bird THOMAS, sheriff, produced commission of J. C. JONES,
Governor...Samuel W. ROBERSON for Justice of the Peace
of Bledsoe County...qualified.

January Session 1842

P. 20 Present on the bench: William BROWN, Joel WHEELER,
Alexander LAMB, John M. BEATTY, J. M. REVICE, Burrell LEA,
Aron SCHOOLFIELD, Thomas J. ROGERS, John F. GREER, Isaac
ROBERSON, William G. DALTON, James ORME, Joseph HICKSON,
Samuel W. ROBERSON and Birum HEARD, Esqr.

Jury of View: Joseph MCDOWELL, William MCDOWELL,
Thomas SMITH, William FARMER, and William BROWN...to
view an alteration in the public road leading from
William WORTHINGTONs up the Cumberland Mountain...
presented report...ordered alterations be made.

p. 21 Voted unanously to allow James A. TULLOSS, Clerk

.the sum of $47.25 for services rendered as such Clerk
from 1 Jan 1841 to 1 Jan 1842.

Sum of $15.25 allowed Willaim C. NORWOOD for guarding the
Jail 21 days and nights in July and August 1841

Sum of $29.25 allowed Willaim H. MOORE for guarding the
Jail 39 nights and days in July and August 1841

James A. TULLOSS, clerk, produced settlement made with
James SKILLERN and A. M. ANDERSON, administrators of
estate of John HENNIGAR, deceased...inspected...ordered
spread on record

James A. TULLOS, clerk, produced settlement made with
Isaac ROBERSON, guardian of the minor heirs of William
LEA, deceased...inspected..ordered spread on record

P. 22   Jas. T. NANNY allowed sum of $6.00 for guarding Jail 8
days and nights in July & August 1841 ...David D. CARDER
allowed $4.87 for 9 nights and 4 days, same period

A. J. HOODENPYLE, former Clerk of Circuit Court, allowed
sum of $1.50 for furnishing a record book for office

Bill of Cost for $64.32 in case of Aron SCHOOLFIELD,
Kinsey SMITH, Isaac STEPHENS, James ROBERSON, Jonathan
WHITESIDE vs The Justice of the peace for Bledsoe County

P. 23   The vote being taken on allowing the above names, and it
was determined in the affirmative unnamously.

James LOYD appointed Treasurer of the poor house for the
year 1842...entered into bond...Matthew PENDERGRASS
appointed Superintendant of the poor house, for the year
1842..entered into bond

State   )   Following allowed $2.00 each for
vs   )   serving two days as Jurors in above
John FIRBUSH   )   cause: James M. REVICE, Andrew THOMAS
James THROPSHIRE   )   Sam FINLEY, Andrew MCDONOUGH, Joseph
    &   )   F. REID, Malcum OWENS, Jeremiah WALKER
Sarah FIRBUSH   )   William S. BROWN, Thomas GANAWAY,
                         Calvin J. MCDONOUGH, John O. JOHNSON.
                         & George RAWLINGS

James BILLINGSLEY appointed overseer of road in room of
Landy SHERLEY.

P. 24   James SKILLERN appointed overseer of road in room of
John CRAWFORD...Charles LOVING appointed in room of
William NESBIT...Hugh PIKE, in stead of James H. FOSTER

Biram HEARD commissioned Justice of the peace..qualified

James LOYD, on of the commissioners of Revinew returned
settlement made with William WALKER, County Trustee...
inspected, ordered to be spread on record

P. 25 The vote being taken on allowing James LOYD, William
FOSTER, commissioners, the sum of $9.00 for settling
with HOODENPYLE, HICKS, TULLOSS, clerks and also to
James LOYD and Martain A. SMITH for settling with the
Executors of Samuel S. STORY, deceased the sum of $2.50
each...affirmative

Jas. LOYD, Treasurer of the poor house allowed $10.00
and Isaac ROBERSON and Right JOHNSON, Commissioners
$5.00 each

James LOYD, Isaac L. ANDERSON, and Right JOHNSON
appointed Commissioners of the poor house for the
ensuing year.

John F. GREER appointed revinew Commissioner in the place
of Wiley REDWINE in the 2nd District

P. 26 Allowance of $1.00 each for every day they attended
court for the year 1841 to Aron SCHOOLFIELD, Daniel F.
COCKE and John M. BEATTY

John M. BEATTY appointed Chairman of court for present
year...Aron SCHOOLFIELD, William BROWN and Burrell LEA
appointed a court corum for present year

Bird THOMAS as sheriff allowed 3 months from this date
to collect and pay over taxes for the purpose for the
court house, that he pay said taxes over to the Trustee,
instead of Thomas CRUTCHFIELD

Margaret PAINE allowed the sum of $20.00 for keeping
Sarah MCCAUL for twelve months, to be paid every 3 months

P. 27 William BROWN and Aron SCHOOLFIELD appointed
Commissioners of revinew to settle with the Clerk and
County Trustee for present year

David GRAHAM appointed overseer of road in stead of
Fielding NARAMORE...Henry HORN apponted in stead of
William HIXSON.

William L. BROWN allowed $5.00 for serving as
commissioner on the poor house in year 1839

Ordered that the following taxes be Levied and assessed
for the present year: On every $100 worth of property
for cents for County purposes. On every and each White
Poll 18 3/4 cents for county purposes, on each and
P. 28 every Merchant for $1000 worth of Capital $1.50 for

county purposes, on each show $50 for County purposes, each
tavern $100 for county purposes...Poor house tax: on
every $100 two cents..9¢, court house tax, every White
poll 43 3/4 cents (note: seems to repeat some items)

Jury of View: Burrell LEA, John M. BEATTY, Reuben
BROWN, Martin A. SMITH, and Isaac L. ANDERSON...to view
alteration in road passing by Samuel BILLINGSLEY to
Pikeville commencing near said BILLINGSLEY house, and
to unite near the top of Hill towards Pikeville ...
report of Jury confirmed, alterations allowed

P. 29 A. J. MCCULLY appointed overseer of public street in
town of Pikeville in room and stead of John W. CHAMBERS

Byram HEARD returned inventory and amount of sales of the
estate of David SMITH deceased..ordered spread on record

On application of Joshua BROWN and petition of 58 persons,
appearing said BROWN is now afflicted by bodily injury
and infirmity...said BROWN entitled to the privilege of
Hawling and Pedling in the County without licence

P. 30 Jury of View: John GREEN, John HALL, Thomas F. BARNETT,
Hubbard BLAYLOCK, John CAMPBELL, Hiriam J. STONE and
Henry DUGGER..to mark out a 2nd class road commencing at
the bridge on on bee_creek in what is called the Crackers
Neck road passing from thence, to intersect the valley
road, on the north side of sequatchie creek

Order made at April term for Jury of View revived. Those
appointed: W. G. GREER, John F. GREER, J. M. REVICE,
William RENFRO, Joseph B. MCCLENDON, Henderson CONLEY,
and James D. HEDGCOTH...to mark out road commencing at
top of Mountain above Craven SHERILLS , to intersect
the Gardens road west of J. M. REVICE

P. 31 Ordered that the line between the 1st and 2nd districts
altered leacing the road at Henderson CONLEYs running due
east course to the top of the Mountain thence with the
extreme highth of Mountain to James HEDGCOTHs, including
said HEDGCOTHS in the first District, thence to the
Crab orchard road

Court appropriated $150.00 to be paid to James P.
THOMPSON for a fee...for a suit in Chancery court...
John M. BEATTY, Chairman vs Thomas CRUTCHFIELD, et al

P. 32 Jury of View: Joseph MCDOWELL, William MCDOWELL,
Thomas MOYERS, Thomas SMITH, and John HANKINS...to view
alteration in road commencing at the spring branch of
Jesse BROWNs and intersecting the old road at or near
the house where William IVITT formerly resided

Ordered that the hands living on the land of George
OXSHER be and are compelled to work on the road that
Aron SCHOOLFIELD is overseer...James WALKER, overseer,
and the hands under him are compelled to work the road
untill it intersects the road passing from TOLLETTs
Mill up the mountain

William WALKER, County Trustee, to pay Pleasant VERNON
the sum of 62½ cents for amount paid by him as poll
tax, when he was exempt

A. M. ANDERSON appointed guardian for the minor heirs of
John HENNIGAR, deceased...entered into bond...

James A. TULLOSS, administrator of the estate of
William HENSON, deceased, allowed untill next term to
return inventory and amount of sales of said estate.

February Session 1842

P. 34   Present on bench: Aron SCHOOLFIELD, William BROWN and
         Burrell LEA, Esqr, Isaac ROBERSON

         James A. TULLOSS, administrator of the estate of William
         HENSON, deceased presented inventory & amount of sales...
         inspected by court...ordered spread on record

         James A. TULLOSS, Clerk produced settlement made with
         Isaac ROBERSON, guardian of minor heirs of William GREER,
         deceased...inspected...ordered spread on record

P. 35   Settlement with Robert OWENS, administrator of the estate
         of William GREER, deceased, inspected, ordered spread
         on record

         Settlement of Benjamin LOWDEN, Administrator of estate of
         James LOWDEN, deceased, inspected, ordered spread on record

         Amos SIMMONS appointed overseer of road in stead of
         Henry DUGGER

         John TOLLETT appointed administrator of estate of G. W.
         TOLLETT...gave bond, was qualified

         John B. CROZIER appointed overseer of road in stead of
         Jesse STANDIFER

P. 36   Bird THOMAS, Sheriff produced commission from James C.
         JONES, Governor...John M. BILLINGSLEY, a Justice of the
         Peace...was qualified

         G. W. TOLLETT departed this life intestate...PHeaby
         TOLLETT, widow and relict...James ORME, Charles K.

SHERILL, and Joseph DORTON appointed commissioners to set apart assets necessary for support of said widow and her family...

P. 37   Application of Lucy DORIS, widow and relict of William DORIS, deceased...James HICKSON appointed administrator of estate of said DORIS...entered into bond...qualified

Azariah BARNETT appointed overseer of road in room and stead of David HORN...William ROGERS appointed overseer of road in room and stead of Jeremiah WALKER...Matthew PENDERGRASS appointed in stead of John B. CROZIER

P. 38   William H. DORIS departed this life intestate...Joel WHEELER, John MCWILLIAMS, Ephriam WELCH appointed commissioners to set apart assets necessary for the support of widow and her family

Francis HUGHS appointed overseer of road in room and stead of Hardy LASETER...Charles WALLS appointed in stead of Charles C. STRANAHAN

P. 39   Satisfactory evidence presented to Court that Francis HUGHS was a pensioner of the United States at the rate of $51.66 per annum, that he was resident of Bledsoe County, State of Tennessee, that he died in county aforesaid on 25th day of January 1841, left no widow, left four children his heirs whose names are John HUGHS, Margaret HUGHS, Ingabow HIXSON and Rebecca HIXSON...only heirs at law known to be living...ordered that the Clerk certify foregoing facts for benefit of said heirs

Ordered that the treasurer of the poor house pay to John M. BEATTY sum of $12.56 for money expended by him for support of Sarah KEENER

March Session 1842   March 7, 1842

P. 40   Present on the bench: Aron SCHOOLFIELD, John M. BEATTY, William BROWN, Burrell LEA, James ORME, John BILLINGSLEY Esqr, Samuel ROBERSON, Will L. DALTON, & Isaac ROBERSON

John TOLLETT, Administrator of estate of G. W. TOLLETT, returned inventory and amount of taxes...inspected, ordered spread on record

G. J. HOLDEN tendered his resignation as constable in 3rd District...received by Court

James A. TULLOSS, Clerk, produced a settlement with Jane ROGERS, Guardian of minor heirs of Frederick J. ROGERS, deceased...inspected, ordered to be spread on record

P. 41   James A. TULLOSS produced settlement made with James ALLEN,
         Guardian of minor heirs of Thomas INGRAM, deceased...
         inspected by Court, ordered spread on record

         James A. TULLOSS, Clerk, produced settlement made with
         John HUTCHESON, guardian of minor heirs of Joseph PETERS,
         deceased...inspected, ordered spread on record

         Samuel MCREYNOLDS appointed overseer of road from his
         residence to the branch at John LEAs...William R. THURMAN,
         overseer, to have all the hands that formally belonged to
         Pleasant VERNON, below the Lot line No. 8 & 9...Pleasant
         VERNON to oversee work from Samuel MCREYNOLDS house to
         Pikeville, with the balance of hands that belonged to him

P. 42   John KNIGHT appointed overseer of road in room and stead
         of Elijah KILGORE

         This day James ORME, Charles SHERILL and Joseph DENTON (?)
         -         on page 36) to set apart one years provision to
         Pheaby TOLLETT, widow of Wilson TOLLETT, deceased...Report:
         We have proceeded to set apart...so much of the crop and
         provisions on hand as will be of sufficient in our opinion
         to support her and her family one year from the death of
         her husband...the following articles, to-wit:
         100 bushels of corn; 400 lbs of Pork; 1 cow and calf; all
         the flax and wood; 300 binds of fodder; $3 for salt and
         leather. Ordered by the court that the above be invested
         in her absolutely.

P. 43   Samuel OXSHEER produced in open court, certificate from
         A. H. COULTER, coroner of Bledsoe County, that said
         OXSHEER had been elected constable.for 2 years, in 3rd
         District...entered into bond...took oath... Bond recorded
         ...$4,000.00...Securities: John TOLLETT, James ORME

         Following allowed sum of $5.00 for taking in the taxable
         property and poll in their several districts for 1842:
         Peter D. WILCOX, John F.GREER, Burrell LEA, William
         BROWN, John BILLINGSLEY, Samuel W. ROBERSON, Aron SCHOOL-
         FIELD, Isaac ROBERSON, Alexander LAMB, and Joel WHEELER.

         A. H. COULTER, coroner, allowed sum of $5.00 for holding
         an inquest over the body of a dead man, by the name of
         Henry GRASON

         Application of James P. SPRING...intention to apply for a
         license to practice law...has attained the age of 21 years,
         has been a citizen of Bledsoe County for twelve months,
         a good and worthy citizen, man of honest morality and
         probity...ordered same be certified.

April Session 1842   April 4, 1842

P. 46 Present on bench:John M. BEATTY, John M. BILLINGSLEY,
William FOSTER, Isaac ROBERSON, William L. DALTON, Burrell
LEA, Wiley REDWINE, William BROWN, James ORME, Samuel W.
ROBERSON, John BILLINGSLEY, Joel WHEELER.

Jury of View appointed for alteration in the public road
commencing on the line between John SWAFFORD and
Elizabeth ORME and running to intersect the old road near
Thomas PRATER: Burrell LEA, Jas. ORME, William PAYNE,
Thomas PRATER and John F. GREER

Ordered by the court that the hands on the East side of
Sequatchie Creek at Tolletts Mill so as to include
Esq. PAYNE and the cow spring then running on the north
side of GOTTs spring branch be alloted to work under
John HICKS, overseer

P. 47 Jury of View to mark out a road commencing at the top of
the Mountain above Craven SHERELL and running to intersect
the gardens road case of James W. REVICE

Allowance of $9.12½ to James A. TULLOSS, Clerk from
1 Jany to 1 Monday of April 1842 for services rendered

The State   )
   vs   )
John PHELPS   )   Peace warrants
Came the defendant, moved the court to be discharged
...answer a charge of the state and in the meantime
keep the peace...State fails and refuses to further
prosecute...defendant go hence thereof discharged...
Elizabeth PHELPS was prosecutor, charge against deft
is frivelous and malicious...she, ordered to pay costs

Certificate of A. H. COULTER, coroner of Bledsoe County,
that following were elected constables on 5 March 1842:
James D. HEDGCOTH, 1st Dist; Thomas B. GREER, 2nd;
Robert DWIGGINS, 4th; Jonathan ACUFF, 5th; James T.
NANNY, and David D. CARDER for the 6th; Audley M.
P. 49 ANDERSON, 7th; Hugh M. BOYD, 8th, Ephraim NELSON, 9th.
Said constables-elect entered into court, entered into
bonds, security approved...each took an oath to support
the Constitution of the United States and the State of
Tennessee and an oath against Duelling and an oath of
office.

Pages 50-58 contain bonds of above constables.
Their securities are as follows:
James D. HEDGCOTH --John HEDGECOTH, James ARMS,
                     Jno. M. BEATTY
   Thomas B. GREER--   John F. GREER, James ORME
   Robert DWIGGINS--   William BRADFORD, James L. SCHOOLFIELD

Jonathan ACUFF-- J. DORSEY, James WORTHINGTON
David D. CARDER--Bird THOMAS, J. DORSEY
James T. NANNY---J. DORSEY, Bird THOMAS
A. M. ANDERSON---William L. BROWN, John SKILLERN
Hugh M. BOYD------B. F. BRIDGMAN, Isaac ROBERSON, E.M. BOYD
Ephraim NELSON---Joseph HIXSON, G. H. BILLINGSLEY

P. 59   Thomas TURNER produced certificate of election as
        constable of 10th district for next two years...
        entered into bond, took oaths..Securities: Byram HEARD,
        James A. TULLOSS, E. M. BOYD, S. C. STANDEFER

        William WALKER produced certificate of election , has been
        elected Trustee for ensuing two years...entered into bond,
        took oath...Securities: J. BRIDGMAN, Isaac ROBERSON

        Bird THOMAS produced certificate of election...Sheriff
        for next two years...entered into bond, took oath...
        Securities: James ORME, Jas. L. SCHOOLFIELD...on three
        bonds, $4,000.00, $2,000.00, $12,000.00

P. 66   John THOMAS produced certificate of election as Clerk of
        Bledsoe County for term of four years...three bonds///
        Securities: Right JOHNSON, James ORMES, Jeremiah DORSEY.

P. 70   Following elected Justices of the Peace: Joseph B.
        McCLENDON, George DAWSON, Wetherston S. GREER, John F.
        GREER, James ORME, William PAINE, John M. BEATTY, William
        BROWN, Samuel RANKIN, William L. BROWN, Samuel W. ROBERSON,
        Jonathan WHITESIDE, Elisha KIRKLIN, William FOSTER,
        William R. THURMAN, Barnabas THOMAS, Joseph HIXSON,
        Samuel H. HUNTER, Joel WHEELER, and Biram HEARD...each
        duly sworn by John M. BEATTY...said BEATTY and Jonathan
        WHITESIDE, sworn and qualified by Isaac ROBERSON, Esqr.
        ALL allowed to take oaths except Barnabas THOMAS.

        Came Barnabas THOMAS ...and moved the court to be
        allowed to take the oaths...question taken as to whether
        THOMAS qualified...court voted Yeas, 8; Nays, 11...and
        so the court refused to permit the said Barnabas THOMAS
        to be qualified as Justice of the Peace

        William R. THURMAN produced in open court...instrument
        ..last will and testament of Eli THURMAN, deceased...James
        A. TULLOSS and Thomas MAUZY, witnesses, called...will
        admitted to record

        Elijah HALE appointed overseer of road in room and stead
        of James WALKER...S. D. HARRIS, IN STEAD OF David KNOX

        James A. TULLOSS, Clerk, produced settlement made with
        Jesse H. STANDIFER, administrator of estate of James
        STANDIFER, deceased...inspected, ordered spread on record

        James A. TULLOSS, Clerk, produced settlement made with
        Isaac B. VERNON, administrator of John CLARK, deceased...
        inspected, ordered spread on Record

P. 74   Aron HICKENBOTTUM appointed overseer of road in room and
        stead of John B. CROZIER...James A. THURMAN, in stead of
        William R. THURMAN

        Samuel McREYNOLDS appointed Trustee of the Lafayette
        Academy in the room and stead of Eli THURMAN, deceased

        John HORN produced in open court one wolf scalp...was
        sworn...wolf was over four months old and was killed in
        Bledsoe County...certificate issued

P. 75   George A. MIRES appointed overseer of road in room and
        of William C. MOSS

        Allowance of four dollars to John BILLINGSLEY

        Allowance of $5.12½ to John THOMAS for keeping and
        feeding James ROSE in said Jail...$5.00 to Samuel
        WHITTENBERG for repairing jail...$7.00 to A. H. COULTER,
        Coroner, for holding Elections on 5th day of March 1842

P. 77   Allowed A. H. COULTER sum of $4.25 for funeral expenses
        for buring the Body of Henry GRAYSON over whom an in-
        quest had been holden

        Allowance to Aron SCHOOLFIELD, William BROWN, and Burrell
        LEA, the court corum, for serving from the first Monday
        of January 1842 to first Monday of April 1842, the sum of
        $1.00 per day for each

        John M. BEATTY was duly elected as chairman of court for
        present year...Three of their body were elected as a
        court corum: William FOSTER, Jonathan WHITESIDE, and
        Samuel W. ROBERSON

        Sheriff ordered to summons the following for July Session
        of Circuit Court: Charles LOWERY, Joseph B. McCLENDON,
        W. S. GREER, J. F. GREER, James Orme, Charles K. SHERILL,
        William PAYNE, William BROWN, Robert WORTHING, Thomas SMITH
        Right JOHNSON, Martha A. SMITH, Samuel PARKER, Jonathan
        WHITESIDE, Pleasant VERNON, Samuel W. ROBERSON, William
        FOSTER, William R. THURMAN, Elkary HALL, William HASKEW,
        Thomas J. ROGERS, William HIXSON, John B. CROZIER, James
        ALLEN and J. R. WHEELER and that James D. HEDGECOTH and
        Thomas TURNER constables be summoned to wait on the court.

P. 79 THIS DAY, JOHN HEDGECOTH, ET AL, WHO WERE APPOINTED A JURY OF VIEW AND MARK OUT A ROAD COMMENCING AT CRAVEN SHERRILL, MADE REPORT...LAID OUT ROAD AGREEABLE TO ORDER...JAMES M. REAVICE APPOINTED OVERSEER, WITH THE FOLLOWING HANDS: SAMUEL LAMBRETH AND HIS HANDS, JESSE LAMBRETH, WILLIAM RENFROE, AND HIS HANDS, JOSEPH B. MCCLENDON AND HIS HANDS, JAMES D. HEDGECOTH, WILLIAM KEETON, AND HIS HANDS, PLEASANT ANDERSON, PLEASANT AAND JOHN HEDGECOTH JOHN HEDGECOTH, JUNR AND JAS. S. REAVICE.

ON MOTION OF JOHN THOMAS, CLERK OF THIS COURT, ANDERSON SLOWN? WAS DULY QUALIFIED TO PERFORM DUTIES AS DEPUTY CLERK OF BLEDSOE COUNTY.

ON MOTION OF BIRD THOMAS, SHERIFF OF BLEDSOE COUNTY, JAMES HIXSON AND WILLIAM ORME WAS DULY QUALIFIED TO PERFORM THE DUTIES AS DEPUTY SHERIFF OF BLEDSOE COUNTY.

P. 81 WILLIAM R. THURMAN CAME INTO COURT...MOTION..APPEARING THAT ELI THURMAN, LATELY OF BLEDSOE COUNTY HAS DEPARTED THIS LIFE ...WILL, APPOINTING SAID WILLIAM R. THURMAN HIS SOLE EXECUTOR...ENTERED INTO BOND...DULY QUALIFIED

ORDERED THAT BIRD THOMAS, SHERIFF HAVE UNTIL NEXT TERM TO PAY OVER MONEY ASSESSED FOR THE PURPOSE OF PAYING FOR THE COURTHOUSE.

ORDERED THAT BIRD THOMAS, SHERIFF, BRING TO THE NEXT TERM OF COURT AN ORPHAN CHILD BY THE NAME OF ONIEL? NOW IN THE POSSESSION OF JESSE CARTER TO BE DEALT WITH AS THE COURT MAY THINK PROPER.

P. 83   MAY SESSION 1842

PRESENT ON THE BENCH: JONATHAN WHITESIDE, WILLIAM FOSTER, SAMUEL H. HUNTER, SAMUEL W. ROBERSON, JOHN M. BEATTY, ELISHA KIRKLEN ESQR.

JOHN JENTRY APPOINTED OVERSEER OF ROAD IN ROOM AND STEAD OF PHILIP HUTCHESON

ADAM LAMB APPOINTED GUARDIAN OF JANE READ, MINOR HEIR OF JOEL READ, DECEASED...ENTERED INTO BOND...QUALIFIED

WILLIAM BRIANT AND GEORGE DAWSON QUALIFIED AS JUSTICES OF THE PEACE

P. 84 SATISFACTORY EVIDENCE SUBMITTED TO THE COURT THAT LATAN
SMITH WAS A PENSIONER OF THE UNITED STATES AT THE RATE OF EIGHTY
DOLLARS PER ANNUM, THAT HE WAS A RESIDENT CITIZEN OF MARION
COUNTY AND STATE OF TENNESSEE AND THAT HE DIED IN THE COUNTY AND
STATE AFORESAID ON THE 12TH DAY OF DECEMBER 1840, THAT HE LEFT NO
WIDOW AT HIS DEATH, THAT HE LEFT FOUR CHILDREN HIS HEIRS AT LAW
WHOSE NAMES ARE ARON SMITH, PATSY ROGERS, FORMERLY PATSY SMITH,
MOSES SMITH, AND ELIZABETH STEP, FORMERLY ELIZABETH SMITH, THAT
THEY ARE ALL THE CHILDREN AND HEIRS AT LAW OF THE SAID LATON
SMITH KNOWN TO BE LIVING, THAT THE SAID MOSES SMITH IS A CITIZEN
OF HAMILTON COUNTY. ARON SMITH AND PATSY ROGERS ARE CITIZENS OF
MARION COUNTY, AND THE SAID ELIZABETH STEP A CITIZEN OF BLEDSOE,
ALL OF THE STATE OF TENNESSEE.

WHEREUPON IT IS ORDERED BY THE COURT THAT THE FACTS AFORESAID BE
CERTIFIED BY THE CLERK FOR THE BENEFIT OF THE HEIRS OF THE SAID
LATON SMITH.

ORDERED BY THE COURT THAT JOHN M. BAITY TAKE ANDERSON ONEIL AND
RETURN HIM TO THE NEXT TERM OF COURT.

P. 85 ORDERED THAT NATHAN COULSTON BE BOUND TO ALLAN GREEN
UNTILL HE ARRIVES AT THE AGE OF TWENTY-ONE...THE SAID GREEN TO
GIVE THE SAID COULSTON SIX MONTHS SCHOOLING, TO FEED AND CLOTHE
HIM , AT THE END OF THE TIME GIVE HIM A HORSE WORTH FIFTY DOLLARS
IN TRADE AND TWO SUITS OF PLAIN CLOTHES. HE WILL BE EIGHTEEN THE
LAST DAY OF DECEMBER 1842.

THIS DAY JAMES HIXSON RETURNED INTO COURT AN INVENTORY AND AMOUNT
OF SALE OF THE ESTATE OF WILLIAM DAVIS, DECEASED...INSPECTED BY
COURT, ORDERED TO RECORD.

COURT ELECTED A. H. COULTER CORONER OFR BLEDSOE COUNTY FOR THE
NEXT ENSUING TWO YEARS...TOOK OATHS...ENTERED INTO
BOND...SECURITY APPROVED

P. 86 BOND OF A. H. COULTER RECORDED...BENJAMIN F. BRIDGMAN AND
WILLIAM BROWN, SECURITIES

COURT ELECTED A RANGER FOR BLEDSOE COUNTY...BENJAMIN F.
BRIDGMAN...TOOK OATHS...BOND RECORDED...A. H. COULTER AND SAMUEL
OXSHEER, SECURITIES

AGREEMENT OF ALLEN GREEN WITH COURT, BINDING NATHAN COULSTON, AN
ORPHAN TO SAID GREEN...WITNESS, JONATHAN RILEY

ORDERED BY THE COURT THAT WILLIAM R. THURMAN BE ALLOWED UNTIL THE
NEXT TERM OF COURT TO RETURN AN INVENTORY OF THE ESTATE OF ELI
THURMAN, DECEASED

P. 89   JUNE SESSION 1842

PRESENT ON THE BENCH: JONATHAN WHITESIDE, SAMUEL H. HUNTER,
SAMUEL W. ROBERSON, ELISHA KIRKLIN, WILLAIM FOSTER, AND JOHN
M.BAITY, ESQR

JOHN JOHNSON APPOINTED OVERSEER OF ROAD IN ROOM AND STEAD OF
JOHN MCWILLIAMS, ELIOT H. BOYD IN ROOM OF JOSIAH RAINS...THOMAS
SWAFFORD IN ROOM OF SAMUEL WORTHINGTON...W. RUSSELL IN ROOM OF
WILLIAM KEEDY

ORDERED THAT THE HANDS THAT WORRKED UNDER JAMES ROBERSON,
OVERSEE OF THE PUBLIC ROAD COMMENCING AT THE BRANCH NEAR THE
WIDOW MCREYNOLDS AND WORKED TO THE SPRING BRANCH NEAR HUGH PIKES
BE ALLOTED TO WORK UNDER HUGH PIKE...

WILLAIM R. THURMAN RETURNED INTO COURT INVENTORY OF THE ESTATE OF
ELI THURMAN, DECEASED...INSPECTED BY THE COURT, ORDERED SPREAD ON
RECORD

ELISHA BOULDIN PRODUCED IN OPEN COURT EIGHT WOLF SCALPS...SWORN,
SAYING THEY WERE UNDER FOUR MONTHS OLD AND WERE KILLED IN BLEDSOE
COUNTY...CERTIFICATE ISSUED IN BEHALF OF SAID BOULDIN

P. 91 ORDERED THAT BIRD THOMAS, SHERIFF, BRING TO NEXT TERM OF
COURT TWO ORPHAN BOYS BY THE NAME OF THOMAS SMITH AND JAMES SMITH

ORDERED THAT JOHN M. BEATTY TAKE AN ORPHAN BOY BY THE NAME OF
ANDERSON ONEIL...UNTIL NEXT TERM OF COURT

P. 92   JULY SESSION 1842

PRESENT ON THE BENCH: JONATHAN WHITESIDE, SAMUEL W. ROBERSON,
WILLIAM FOSTER, WILLIAM BROWN, SAMUEL RANKIN, WILLIAM R. THURMAN,
ESQR.

JOHNATHAN WHITESIDE APPOINTED CHAIRMAN OF THE COURT PROTEM

ALLOWANCE OF TWENTY-FIVE DOLLARS MADE TO SYNTHA SPARKS, HALF THE
APPRAISED VALUE OF A STRAY HORSE

ORDERED THAT THE FOLLOWING GENTLEMEN WORK UNDER JAMES
BILLINGSLEY, OVERSEER: NICHOLAS ACUFF, WILLIAM ACUFF, ROBERT
ACUFF, WILLIAM THOMAS, MARTIN A. SMITH, JOHN M. BILLINGSLEY,
JOSEPH POLARD, THOMAS BOMIN, JOB BOMIN, WILLIAM BROCK, FRA. NED
AND TRAVIS SIMMONS.

ORDERED THAT THE ROAD LEADING FROM THE WIDOW MCREYNOLDS AND
RUNNING TO ISAAC ROBERSONS BE ALTERED FROM A SECOND CLASS ROAD TO
A THIRD CLASS ROAD

P. 93 ALLOWANCE OF $3.00 TO SAMUEL WHITTENBURG FOR REPAIRING
JAIL OF BLEDSOE COUNTY

ABB HARRISON APPOINTED OVERSEER OF ROAD IN ROOM AND STEAD OF
BRIANT MERRIMAN

JONATHAN WHITESIDE APPOINTED TRUSTEE OF THE LAFAYETTE ACADEMY IN
ROOM AND STEAD OF SCOTT TERRY

P. 95 ORDERED THAT PUBLIC ROAD FROM PETER SWAFFORDS TO TOLLETTS
MILL FORMERLY KEPT UP BY ONE OVERSEER BE DIVIDED...ELIGA HALL
APPOINTED OVERSEER OF THE UPPER END WITH THE FOLLOWING HANDS:
OWEN RECTOR, B. A. HALL, JAMES WALKER, PLEASANT WRIGHT, JOSEPPH
HIDER, ELI BROWN, NELSON SCISSOM, ARON SWAFFORD, WILLIAM ONEIL,
ELIGA HAIL, AND WASHINGTON HAIL...THE DIVIDING LINE TO RUN FROM
SCHOOLFIELDS MEETING HOUSE TO THOMAS HAILS, LEAVING HAIL ON THE
UPPER END. FURTHER ORDERED THAT JOEL HALE BE APPOINTED OVERSEER
OF THE LOWER END OF SAID ROAD...FOLLOWING GENTLEMEN APPOINTED TO
WORK UNDER HIM: RICHARD COULTER, NASON SWAFFORD, JOHN PRAYTOR,
HAMPTON SALES, G. W. MILLARD, JEFFERSON CANADA, GEORGE H. FINLEY,
JAMES L. SCHOOLFIELD, JOHN CANADA, AND THOMAS SWAFFORD, JUNR.

ALLOWANCE TO MISTRESS PAYNE...SUM OF FIVE DOLLARS FOR KEEPING
SARAH MCCALL, A PAUPER DECD. AT HER HOUSE

P. 96 ALLOWANCE TO DR. THOMAS MANZER...FIVE DOLLARS FOR MEDICAL
AID TO SARAH MCCALL

$47.65 RECD. PIKEVILLE JULY 4TH 1842 OF JAMES A. TULLOSS FORMER
CLERK OF THE COUNTY COURT OF BLEDSOE COUNTY...REVENUE COLLECTED
BY HIM...FROM 1 SEPT 1841 TO 4 APRIL 1842, THE TIME HE WENT OUT

OF OFFICE...S/WILLIAM WALKER, COUNTY TRUSTEE

P. 97 $19.25...RECEIVED OF JAMES A. TULLOSS, FORMER CLERK OF
BLEDOSE COUNTY...MONEY COLLECTED FOR THE USE OF THE COURT HOUSE,
ABOVE DATES...S/WILLIAM WALKER, COUNTY TRUSTEE

ALLOWANCE OF EIGHT DOLLARS AND THIRTY-SEVEN AND A HALF CENTS, FOR
COST IN CIRCUIT COURT

ALLOWANCE TO CRAVEN SHERILL, FORMER SHERIFF OF BLEDSOE
COUNTY...SUM OF THIRTY DOLLARS FOR SERVICES RENDERED

P. 98 ALLOWANCE OF THIRTY DOLLARS TO JAMES A. TULLOSS, FORMER
CLERK OF THIS COURT, FOR EXOFFICES FEES FOR FOUR YEARS

P. 99 WILLIAM FOSTER, GUARDIAN OF MINOR HEIRS OF DAVID POINER,
DECEASED, PRESENTED REPORT OF ASSETS OF SAID HEIRS...BOND OF SAID
FOSTER...SECURITIES, JAMES A. TULLOSS, WILLIAM HASKEW

P. 100 JOSEPH HIXSON, GUARDIAN OF MINOR HEIRS OF JOHN HIXSON,
DECEASED, READ IN OPEN COURT HIS REPORT OF THE ASSETS OF THE SAID
HEIRS IN HIS HANDS...ENTERED INTO BOND...SECURITIES: WILLIAM
WALKER AND WILLIAM BRIANT...AMOUNT OF $1200.00...APPROVED

P. 101 ISAAC ROBERSON, GUARDIAN OF MINOR HEIRS OF WILLIAM GREER,
DECEASED, RETURNED INTO COURT HIS REPORT OF ASSETS OF SAID
HEIRS...ENTERED INTO BOND, $3,000.00...SECURITIES, WILLIAM
WALKER, WILLAIM FOSTER...APPROVED

P. 102 ISAAC ROBERSON , GUARDIAN OF MINOR HEIRS OF WILLIAM LEE,
DECEASED, RETURNED INTO COURT HIS REPORT OF ASSETS OF SAID
HEIRS...ENTERED INTO BOND, $400.00...SECURITIES, WILLIAM WALKER,
WILLIAM FOSTER...APPROVED

P. 103   THE STATE OF TENNESSEE)
              VS   )
         WILLIAM RANDOLPH   ) PEACE WARRANT

EVIDENCE EXAMINED...CONSIDERED BY COURT THAT DEFENDANT IS NOT
GUILTY AS THEREIN CHARGED...APPEARING PROSECUTION FRIVILOUS AND
MALICIOUS, AND THAT JOHN MOORE IS THE PROSECUTOR...MOORE TO PAY
ALL COSTS

NATHAN COULSTON, A CERTAIN ORPHAN BOY, BOUND TO ALLEN GREEN AS AN

APPRENTICE, HAS WITHOUT REASONABLE CAUSE RUN AWAY...ORDERED THAT
SAID GREEN IS RELEASED FROM ALL LIABILITY

PUBLIC ROAD HAVING BEEN ESTABLISHED AT OCTOBER SESSION, 1840...NO
OVERSEER EVER APPOINTED...ORDERED THAT ROBERT FRANKLIN BE
APPOINTED OVERSEER OF SAID ROAD...MARKED AND LAID OUT FROM TOP OF
CUMBERLAND MOUNTAIN AT SHERRELLS GAP AND INTERSECTING OFFESERS
TURN PIKE ROAD NEAR BAZZELL HEDGECOTHS...HANDS TO WORK ROAD:
ABNER HARRIS, JAMES SUTTON, WILLIAM SUTTON, BAZZEL HEDGCOTH,
JAMES MCCLENDON AND JOHN SUTTON.

P. 105 ORDER AT MAY SESSION, DIRECTING THE SHERIFF OF BLEDSOE
COUNTY TO PAY OVER, WHEN COLLECTED, THE AMOUNT OF TAX ASSESSED
FOR THE PURPOSE OF PAYING FOR THE BUILDING OF THE COURT HOUSE IN
THIS COUNTY, TO THOMAS CRUTCHFIELD, THE CONTRACTOR...SAID MONEY
NOT PAID...ORDERED THAT LAST MENTIONED ORDER BE DECLARED
VOID...SHERIFF TO PAY OVER SAID TAXES TO TRUSTEE

AT JANUARY SESSION, 1842 OF THIS COURT, ORDER WAS MADE
AUTHORIZING THE COUNTY TRUSTEE TO PAY TO JAMES P. THOMPSON THE
SUM OF $150.00 FOR HIS SERVICES AS ATTORNEY IN CAUSE PENDING IN
CHANCERY COURT...APPEARING ORDER IS ILLEGAL...DECLARED VOID

P. 106 APPEARING THERE ARE DIVERS GUARDIANS IN THE COUNTY OF
BLEDSOE WHO HAVE FAILED TO APPEAR AND RENDER STATEMENTS AND RENEW
BONDS...CLERK OF CXOURT TO ISSUE NOTICE TO EACH GUARDIAN TO
APPEAR AT NEXT TERM OF COURT

P. 107 JACOB NEWMAN APPOINTED OVERSEER OF ROAD IN ROOM AND STEAD
OF JOHN M. SMITH

ON APPLICATION OF WILLIAM L. DALTON, BIRD PANKEY CAME INTO COURT
AND WAS QUALIFIED AS DEPICTS ENTRITAKE

P. 108   AUGUST SESSION 1842

COURT ELECTED SURVEYOR FOR COUNTY FOR NEXT FOUR YEARS...ARON
SCHOOLFIELD...GAVE BOND...QUALIFIED

COURT ELECTED ONE OF THEIR OWN BODY AS CHAIRMAN TO FILL THE
VACANCY OCCASIONED BY THE DEATH OF JOHN M. BEATTY...WILLIAM
FOSTER

LEWIS KEEDY RELEASED FROM PAYMENT OF POLL TAX FOR YEAR 1842

LEWIS KEEDY ALSO RELEASED FROM PAYMENT OF POLL TAX FOR YEAR 1841

JAMES ROGERS PRODUCED IN OPEN COURT REPORT OF ASSETS OF ESTATE OF
FREDERICK J. ROGERS...ENTERED INTO BOND, $800.00, SECURITIES,
WILLIAM WALKER, WILLIAM ROGERS, JOSEPH HIXSON...APPROVED

ARON SCHOOLFIELD, GUARDIAN OF DAVID SCHOOLFIELD, ENTERED INTO
BOND, $50.00, SECURITIES, WILLIAM WALKER AND JOSEPH
HIXSON...APPROVED

P. 111 ORDERED THAT JAMES COX BE BOUND UNTO ARON SWAFFORD BY THE
CONSENT OF HIS MOTHER UNTILL HE ARRIVES AT THE AGE OF EIGHTEEN
THE 25TH DAY OF SEPTEMBER NEXT...SWAFFORD ENTERED INTO BOND...COX
TO LIVE AND WORK WITH SWAFFORD UNTIL AGE OF TWENTY YEARS...THOMAS
SWAFFORD, SECURITY

COURT APPOINTS FOLLOWING AS JURY OF VIEW: WILLIAM HERD, PHILIP
HOOTS, JOHN MANSFIELD, A. B. WOOTON, JACOB TEETERS, AND ROBERT
ORMES...TO WORK OUT ROAD COMMENCING AT OR NEAR JOHN HERDS...TO
INTERSECT ROAD AT KELLY FISH TRAP LEADING FROM SAVAGES TURNPIKE
TO CHATTANOOGA...MAKE REPORT NEXT TERM

WILLIAM L. BROWN ALLOWED FOUR DOLLARS FOR ATTENDING AS A JUROR AT
MARCH TERM OF CIRCUIT COURT

THOMAS SWAFFORD JR. APPOINTED OVERSEER OF ROAD IN ROOM AND STEAD
OF ROBERT LEA...WORK DOWN TO REUBIN BROWN WOODLAND PASTURE AND
HAVE THE HANDS ON THE UPPER END INCLUDING JONATHAN CLARK AND
WORKING UP TO THE MOUNTAIN LEAVING JAMES BROWN ON THE CORNER END
OF THE ROAD

P. 113 EZEKIEL CURTIS APPOINTED OVERSEER OF ROAD ON LOWER END OF
ROAD ON WHICH ROBERT LEA HAS FORMERLY BEEN OVERSEER FROM REUBIN
BROWN WOODLAND PASTURE TO SAMUEL WORTHINGTON

COURT PROCEED TO TAKE VOTE WHETHER WILLIAM WALKER, TRUSTEE SHOULD
RECEIVE FROM BIRD THOMAS, SHERIFF, ALABAMA MONEY FOR TAXES
COLLECTED...NAYS, 11...DETERMINED BY COURT THAT TRUSTEE RECEIVED
NOTHING BUT TENNESSEE MONEY...FOR YEAR 1841

P. 114 BIRD THOMAS, SHERIFF SHALL NOT TAKE ANY KIND OF MONEY
EXCEPT TENNESSEE MONEY OR ITS EQUIVILENT FOR TAXES FOR YEAR 1842

SURVEYOR ELECTED FOR FOUR YEARS IN ROOM AND STEAD OF JOHN M.

BEATTY, DECEASED...ARON SCHOOLFIELD...QUALIFIED, ENTERED INTO
BOND, $25,000.00...SECURITIES, SAMUEL MCREYNOLDS, E. H. BOYD, AND
ISAAC ROBERSON

ORDERED THAT THE SHERIFF SUMMONS THE FOLLOWING GENTLEMEN TO
ATTEND AS JURORS FOR THE CIRCUIT COURT FOR BLEDSOE COUNTY AT
NOVEMBER TERM: GEORGE DAWSON, CHARLES LOWERY, ISAAC STEPHENS,
ROBERT WORTHINGTON, JOHN TOLLETT, WILLIAM WORTHINGTON, WILLIAM
BROWN, JOSEPH MCDOWEL, JOHN HUTCHESON, A. B. CARNES, JOHN HALL,
SAMUEL MCREYNOLDS, WM. VERNON, ELISHA KIRKLIN, JAMES F. LOYD,
VALENTINE SPRINGS, E. H. BOYD, WILLIAM BRIANT, BUCKNOR HOWARD,
JOSEPH HIXSON, ADAM LAMB, JONATHAN POPE, A. C. WHEELER, AND THAT
A. H. ANDERSON, NATHANIEL BRISTOE, JAMES WALKER, AND DAVID D.
CARDER BE SUMMONED TO WAIT ON THE COURT.

P. 118   SEPTEMBER SESSION   1842

JOHN THOMAS, CLERK, PRODUCED IN OPEN COURT SETTLEMENT MADE BY HIM
WITH MARY MASSEE, GUARDIAN OF MINOR HEIRS OF RICHARD MASSESS,
DECEASED...INSPECTED.. ORDERED TO RECORD

SETTLEMENT WITH JANE ROGERS, GUARDIAN OF MINOR HEIRS OF FREDERICK
J. ROGERS, DECEASED...INSPECTED BY COURT, ORDERED TO RECORD

THIS DAY BARNABAS THOMAS TENDERED HIS RESIGNATION AS JUSTICE OF
THE PEACE FOR THE EIGHTH DISTRICT OF BLEDSOE COUNTY...ACCEPTED

JURY OF VIEW APPOINTED AT LAST TERM OF COURT ALLOWED UNTIL NEXT
TERM TO MAKE REPORT

P. 119   VALENTINE SPRING APPOINTED OVERSEER OF PUBLIC ROAD
BETWEEN SEQUATCHY BRIDGE AND ARON SCHOOLFIELD BLACKSMITH SHOP
WHAT HANDS LIVE ON SAID SPRINGS LAND TO WORK UNDER HIM

P. 120   OCTOBER SESSION   1842

PRESENT ON BENCH: ELISHA KIRKLIN, SAMUEL H. HUNTER, GEORGE
DAWSON, SAMUEL RANKIN, BYRAM HEARD, JONATHAN WHITESIDE, JOHN F.
GREER, WETHERSTON S. GREER, WHEELER, HIXSON, FOSTER, PAYNE,
BROWN, ORME

ALLOWANCE OF $2.75 TO ELISHA KIRKLIN FOR FURNISHING SHARE FOR
PAUPER

JAMES A. TULLOSS AND SAMUEL RANKIN APPOINTED TO SETTLE WITH J. R. WHEELER, ADMINISTRATOR OF ELISHA THOMAS DECD AND MAKE REPORT THIS TERM OF COURT

ALLOWANCE OF $16.50 TO JAMES T. KENNY FOR GUARDING THE JAIL OF BLEDSOE COUNTY...ALLOWANCE FOR SAME TO JOHN B. THOMAS

ALLOWANCE OF $7.00 TO BIRD THOMAS FOR MONEY EXPENDED BY HIM FOR BRINGING JA ES FOSTER BACK TO THE JAIL

ORDERED THAT NICHOLAS NANNYS STOCK MARK BE RECORDED THE MARK OF A CROSS OVER THE LEFT YEAR A SWALLOW FORK AND UNDER BIT IN THE WRIGHT

JAMES A. TULLOSS APPOINTED OVERSEER OF ROAD IN ROOM AND STEAD OF SCOT TERRY...JOHN MANSFIELD APPOINTED IN ROOM OF WILLIAM S. ROGERS...JACOB HORN IN ROOM OF HESEKIAH BURNETT

JAMES M. REAVESS RELEASED AS OVERSEER...HENDERSON CONLEY APPOINTED IN HIS ROOM AND STEAD

ALLOWANCE TO BIRD THOMAS, SHERIFF AND PUBLIC COLLECTOR OF PUBLIC TAXES, THE SUM OF $42.80 FOR DELINQUENTS IN BLEDSOE COUNTY

JOHN KELLY RELEASED FROM PAYING THE HALF APPRAISED VALUE OF A STRAY FILLY

JAMES ROSE RELEASED FROM PAYING POLL TAX FOR YEAR 1841...THOMAS RELEASED FROM PAYMENT FOR SAME YEAR

P. 124 RECEIPT OF WILLIAM WALKER, TRUSTEE...$L7.53 RECEIVED FROM JOHN THOMAS, REVENUE COLLECTED FROM 4TH DAY OF APRIL 1842 TO 1ST SEPT 1842

ALLOWANCE OF $3.00 TO E. H. BOYD AND WILLIAM ROGERS FOR FURNISHING A SLEDGE HAMMER TO WORK ON ROAD

COURT VOTED IN THE AFFIRMATIVE TO TAKE ALABAMA MONEY FROM BIRD THOMAS, SHERIFF FOR TAXES COLLECTED TO PAY FOR THE COURT HOUSE FOR THE YEAR 1841

ALLOWANCE OF $30.00 TO STEPHEN HICKS, CLERK OF THE CIRCUIT COURT
OF BLEDSOE COUNTY

ALLOWANCE OF $3.00 TO JESSE BROWN AND JOHN HINCH, OVERSEERS, FOR
FURNISHING A SLEDGE HAMMER TO WORK ON ROAD

P. 127 JOHN THOMAS, CLERK, PRODUCED IN OPEN COURT SETTLEMENT
MADE WITH JOSEPH HIXSON, GUARDIAN OF THE MINOR HEIRS OF JOHN
HIXSON, DECEASED...INSPECTED BY COURT, ORDERED TO RECORD

SETTLEMENT MADE WITH JAMES ORME AND GEORGE F. JONES,
ADMINISTRATORS OF THE ESTATE OF MOSES ORME, DECEASED...INSPECTED
BY COURT, ORDERED TO RECORD

JURY OF VIEW: JOHN MANSFIELD, J. B. EWTON, JACOB TETERS, WILLIAM
HERD, AND PHILIP HOOTS...TO VIEW OUT ROAD COMMENCING AT JOHN
HERDS JR AND RUNNING ROUND JOHN HERD SR. FENCE TO KELLYS FISH TRAP
LEADING FROM SAVAGE TURNPIKE TO CHATTANOOGA...REPORT
RETURNED...FAVORABLE...ORDERED ROAD BE ESTABLISHED...WILLIAM HERD
APPOINTED OVERSEER IN ROOM AND STEAD OF BYRON HERD

P. 128 JAMES A. TULLOSS AND SAMUEL RANKIN MADE SETTLEMENT WITH
J. R. WHEELER, ADMINISTRATOR OF ESTATE OF ELISHA THOMAS,
DECD...EXAMINED BY COURT, ORDERED TO RECORD

P. 129   NOVEMBER SESSION 1842

PRESENT ON BENCH: JONATHAN WHITESIDE, WILLIAM FOSTER, WILLIAM
BRIANT, WILLIAM BROWN, AND SAMUEL HUNTER, ESQR

THIS DAY WETHERSTON S. GREER TENDERED HIS RESIGNATION AS JUSTICE
OF THE PEACE FOR THE 2ND DISTRICT...ACCEPTED

JOHN L. MOIS APPOINTED OVERSEER OF ROAD IN ROOM AND STEAD OF
CHARLES LOOING

ELIZABETH PHELPS APPOINTED ADMINISTRATOR OF JOHN PHELPS,
DECEASED...QUALIFIED, ENTERED INTO BOND, $1,000.00...SECURITIES,
ROBERT BARGER AND TOLOTT BARGER

HENRY THOMAS APPOINTED OVERSEER OF ROAD IN ROOM AND STEAD OF ELI
TURNER

P. 132 JOHN THOMAS, CLERK, PRODUCED SETTLEMENT MADE WITH ISAAC
B. VERNON, ADMINISTRATOR OF ESTATE OF JOHN CLARK...ACCEPTED,
ORDERED TO RECORD

ON APPLICATION OF MARY CLARK, WIDOW OF JOHN CLARK, DECEASED, SHE
IS APPOINTED GUARDIAN OF MINOR HEIRS OF JOHN CLARK,
DECEASED...ENTERED BOND, $400.00, SECURITIES, JONATHAN WHITESIDE
AND ISAAC B. VERNON...CHILDREN OF JOHN CLARK, DECD: DANIEL
CLARK, NANCY CLARK, CAROLINE, JANE AND MAY

P. 134 DECEMBER SESSION   1842

PRESENT ON THE BENCH: ESQ. WHITESIDE, ROBERSON, HUNTER, ORME,
JOHN F. GREER

JONATHAN WHITESIDE APPOINTED CHAIRMAN PROTEM

JAMES ORME, CRAVEN SHERILL AND CHARLES K. SHERILL APPOINTED TO
LAY OFF AND SET APART ONE YEARS PROVISION FOR THE WIDOW
PHELPS...MAKE RETURN NEXT TERM

JONATHAN BILLINGSLEY APPOINTED OVERSEER OF ROAD IN ROOM AND STEAD
OF GEORGE MUNCY...CLAIBIN DEVENPORT APPOINTED IN ROOM OF WILSON,
DECD WITH THE SAME HANDS AND BOUNDS THROUGH SWAGGY COVE AND THAT
WILLIAM HAMILTON WORK ON THE OTHER END TO INTERSECT GEORGE
GORDONS ROAD THAT SAID DEVENPORT WAS OVERSEER OF IN TOLLETS LIFE
TIME

ORDERED THAT THE FOLLOWING NAMED GENTLEMEN ATTEND AS JURORS,
MARCH TERM OF CIRCUIT COURT 1843: CHARLES LOWERY, MORGAN NAVISS,
JOHN F. GREER, WILLIAM LOWDEN, SIMEON SELBY, JAMES STEPHENS,
JAMES ORME, COL. WM. BROWN, PHILIP S. HUTCHESON, SAMUEL RANKIN,
WILLIAM L. BROWN, JONATHAN WHITESIDE, SAMUEL W. ROBERSON,
PLEASANT VERNON, BIRD, HENSON, WM. FOSTER, JOHN LEE, BENJAMIN,
BRIANT, WILLIAM BRIANT, SAMUEL H. HUNTER, WILLIAM HIXSON, JOEL
WHEELER, BYRAM HERD, HUGH PIKE, ISAAC ROBERSON, JEREMIAH DORSY,
AND THAT JAMES L. NAY, AND EPHRIAM NELSON WAIT ON SAID COURT.

ORDERED THAT BIRD THOMAS BRING NANCY NEWBE A PAUPER NOW AT THE
POOR HOUSE AT THE NEXT TERM OF COURT

ORDERED BY THE COURT THAT THE FOLLOWING NAMED GENTLEMEN BE
APPOINTED REVINEW COMMISSIONERS TO TAKE IN A LIST OF TAXABLE
PROPERTY AND POLE IN THE SEVERAL DISTRICTS OF BLEDSOE COUNTY:

        1. GEORGE DAWSON
        2. JOHN F. GREER
        3. JAMES ORME
        4. WILLIAM BROWN
        5. SAMUEL RANKIN
        6. SAMUEL W. ROBERSON
        7. WM. FOSTER
        8. WM. BRIANT
        9. JOSEPH HIXSON
       10. BYRAM HERD

P. 136 THOMAS B. GREER TENDERED HIS RESIGNATION AS CONSTABLE IN
THE 2ND DISTRICT OF BLEDSOE COUNTY...ACCEPTED BY COURT

BOND OF EDWIN BEATTY, $2,000.00...SECURITIES: WILLIAM FARMER AND
JAMES STEPHENS...ADMINISTRATOR OF ESTATE OF JOHN BEATY, DECEASED

P. 138 EDWAIN BEATY APPEARED IN OPEN COURT, WAS QUALIFIED AS
ADMINISTRATOR OF JOHN M. BAITY, DECEASED

ELIZABETH PHELPS, ADMINISTRATRIX OF JOHN PHELPS, DECEASED,
RETURNED IN COURT INVENTORY OF PROPERTY OF SAID JOHN PHELPS,
DECEASED

ISAAC ROBERSON AND SAMUEL H. HUNTER APPOINTED TO LAY OFF AND SET
APART ONE YEARS PROVISION FOR THE WIDOW OF HENRY KINSY, DECD

ON APPLICATION OF SARAH KINSY, WIDOW OF HENRY KINSY, DECD, SHE IS
APPOINTED ADMINISTRATRIX OF ESTATE OF HENRY KINSY,
DECD...QUALIFIED, ENTERED INTO BOND...$50.00...SECURITIES, ISAAC
ROBERSON AND SAMUEL HUNTER (ABSTRACTOR'S NOTE: IN THE BOND THE
SURNAME IS KERSY, AND THE BOND IS SIGNED BY SARAH KERSY.)...SAME
DAY, SARAH KERSY RETURNED AN INVENTORY OF THE ESTATE OF HENRY
KERSY...ACCEPTED, ORDERED TO RECORD

P. 142   JANUARY SESSION 1843   5TH JANUARY 1843

ON THE BENCH THE WORSHIPFUL ESQ. WHITESIDE, COL. ROBERSON,
RANKIN, WM. BROWN, SAM W. ROBERSON, HUNTER, ORME, PAYNE, BRIANT,
WILLIAM L. BROWN, HUTCHESON, HIXSON, GREER, HERD, WHEELER AND
MCCLENDON

JOHN MANNING PRODUCED IN OPEN COURT ONE WOLF SCALP...WOLF, OVER
FOUR MONTHS OLD WHEN KILLED IN BLEDSOE COUNTY...CERTIFICATE
ISSUED

SAMUEL H. HUNTER AND ISAAC ROBERSON, VALENTINE SPRING, AT LAST
TERM OF COURT, APPOINTED TO LAY OFF TO SARAH KEASY, WIDOW, TWELVE
MONTHS PROVISIONS, RETURNED REPORT:

1 OLD COW AND YEARLING	$ 7.00
1 BED & BED STEAD	10.00
1 " " "	6.00
1 PR. STRECHERS & CHEST	1.25
OLD PLATES, KNIVES & FORKS	1.50
OVEN POTS & SKILLETS	2.50
1 PR DRAWING CHAINS	1.00
1 AX	.50
1 COLT	15.00
1/2 OF FLAX WHEEL	1.25
1 SINGLETREE	.50
12 HEAD OF GEESE	____3.00_
AMT.	$49.50

P. 143 JAMES ORME, CRAVEN SHERILL AND CHARLES K. SHERILL,
COMMISSIONERS APPOINTED TO LAY OFF AND SET APART TO ELIZABETH
PHELPS, WIDOW, TWELVE MONTHS PROVISIONS PRESENTED REPORT:

1 COW FOR L2 MONTHS	
50 BUSHELS CORN	
FOR PORK	$8
2 SALT	3
" LEATHER	2

EDWARD BEATY, ADMINISTRATOR OF JOHN M. BEATY RETURNED INVENTORY
OF THE EFFECTS AND ASSETS OF THE ESTATE OF JOHN M. BEATY,
DECEASED...INSPECTED, ORDERED TO BE RECORDED

SAMUEL OXIER CONSTABLE, TENDERED HIS RESIGNATION...RECEIVED

P. 143 WILLIAM SMITH RELEASED FROM PAYING POLL TAX FOR YEAR 1842

JORDAN SMITH APPOINTED OVERSEER IN ROOM AND STEAD OF HENRY HORN

COURT PROCEEDED TO ELECT THREE OF THEIR BODY AS A COURT QUORAM
FOR YEAR 1843: SAMUEL W. ROBERSON, JONATHAN WHITESIDE, WILLIAM
BROWN

WILLIAM FOSTER AND SAMUEL RANKIN APPOINTED COMMISSIONERS TO
SETTLE WITH COUNTY TRUSTEE AND CLERK

WILLIAM P. HAMBLE APPOINTED OVERSEER OF ROAD IN ROOM AND STEAD OF JOHN POPE

THIS DAY MATHY PENDERGRASS PRODUCED IN OPEN COURT REPORT AS SUPERINTENDENT OF POOR HOUSE...INSPECTED, ORDERED TO RECORD

ORDERED THAT LEVI CARTER TAKE NANCY NEWBEE A PAUPER AND KEEP HER SIX MONTHS FOR WHICH HE SHALL HAVE THE SUM OF SEVENTEEN DOLLARS...TREASURY OF POOR HOUSE TO PAY

P. 145 ALLOWANCE MADE TO JAMES LOYD, TREASURER OF POOR HOUSE. SUM OF TEN DOLLARS...SUM OF FIVE DOLLARS TO ISAAC L. ANDERSON, SUPERINTENDENT OF POOR HOUSE

P. 146 ALLOWANCE OF SUM OF FIVE DOLLARS TO RIGHT JOHNSON, SUPERINTENDENT OF POOR HOUSE

ALLOWANCE TO SAMUEL W. ROBERSON , JONATHAN WHITESIDE & WILLIAM FOSTER, COURT QUORUM, THE SUM OF ONE DOLLAR PER DAY EACH FOR SERVING AS SUCH COURT QUORUM

JAMES ORME, COL. WILLIAM BROWN, & MARTIN A. SMITH APPOINTED TO COMMISSION THE POOR HOUSE FOR THE YEAR 1843...APPEARED IN OPEN COURT...QUALIFIED

MARTIN A. SMITH APPOINTED TREASURY OF THE COURT HOUSE FOR YEAR1843...APPEARED, ENTERED INTO BOND...$300.00, SECURITY: WILLIAM WORTHINGTON

P. 148 FOLLOWING APPOINTED TO INQUIRE INTO THE CONDITION OF JOSEPH NEWMAN SON AND DAUGHTER...MAKE REPORT AT NEXT TERM: JAMES ORME, JOHN F. GREER, JOSEPH B. MCCLENDON, WILLIAM S. GREER, WILLIAM RENFRO, CRAVEN SHERILL, JAMES M. REAVIS, JOHN HERD, JAMES WALKER, GEORGE DAWSON, PLEASANT ANDERSON, & CHESTER LOWERY

COL. WILLIAM BROWN ELECTED CHAIRMAN OF COURT FOR YEAR 1843

ON APPLICATION OF BIRD THOMAS, SAMUEL OXSHER APPEARED IN OPEN COURT AND WAS QUALIFIED AS DEPUTY SHERIFF

ALLOWANCE OF $1.15 MADE TO CRAVEN SHERILL, FORMER SHERIFF, FOR COMMISSION ON EXTRA TAX LIST FOR THE YEAR 1843

FOLLOWING TAX LEVIED AND ASSESSED FOR THE YEAR 1843: FOR COUNTY
PURPOSES ON EVERY HUNDRED DOLLARS WORTH OF PROPERTY, 4 CENTS...ON
EACH WHITE POLL 18/11 CENTS FOR COUNTY PURPOSES...ON EACH
MERCHANT FOR EVERY THOUSAND DOLLARS WORTH OF CAPITAL, $1.00...FOR
EACH SHOW $30.00 FOR COUNTY PURPOSES...ON EACH TAVERN, $L.00 FOR
COUNTY PURPOSES...POOR HOUSE TAX: ON EACH $100 WORTH OF PROPERTY,
2 CENTS...COURT HOUSE TAX: ON EACH $100 WORTH OF PROPERTY, 9
CENTS...ON EACH WHITE POLL, 43 2/11 CENTS ...ON EACH THOUSAND
DOLLARS $2.50 ON EACH MERCHANT...ON EACH SHOW, $30...ON EACH
STALION OR JACK THE SEASON PRICE OF ONE MARE

COURT VOTED ALLOWANCE FOR FEES INDORSED IN COUNTY TO JOHN THOMAS,
CLERK, SUM OF THIRTY NINE DOLLARS, EIGHTEEN AND THREE-FOOURTHS
CENTS

P. 150 JOHN THOMAS, CLERK, PRODUCED SETTLEMENT MADE WITH ISAAC
B. HENSON, WILLIAM HENSON AND PETER HOODENPYLE, EXECUTORS OF LAST
WILL AND TESTAMENT OF JONATHAN HENSON, DECEASED...INSPECTED,
ORDERED TO BE PUT ON RECORD

JOHN THOMAS PRODUCED SETTLEMENT MADE WITH ISAAC ROBERSON,
GUARDIAN OF MINOR HEIRS OF WILLIAM GREER, DECEASED...INSPECTED,
ORDERED TO RECORD

ORDERED THAT GILBREATH KELLY BE BOUND UNTO WILLIAM SKILLERN
UNTILL HE ARRIVES AT THE AGE OF TWENTY-ONE...HE IS NOW ELEVEN
YEARS OLD...SKILLERN ENTERED INTO BOND AND AGREEMENT...TO BE
GIVEN A HORSE SADDLE WORTH EIGHTY-FIVE DOLLARS AND EDUCATION
READING WRITING AND ARITHMETIC TO THE RULE OF THREE AND AT THE
EXPIRATION OF HIS TIME, GIVE HIM A GOOD SUIT OF JENES
CLOTHES...WILL ALWAYS FURNISH SAID KELLY SUFFICIENT DIET LODGING
AND WASHING AND APPAREL ...BIRD THOMAS, SECURITY

FOLLOWING APPOINTED TO SUPERINTEND THE REPAIRING OF THE JAIL OF
BLEDSOE COUNTY AND LET OUT REPAIRING OF SAME ON SECOND MONDAY IN
MARCH NEXT TO LOWEST BIDDER: WILLIAM WORTHINGTON, A. B. CARNES,
BIRD THOMAS, PETER HOODENPYL, SAMUEL MCREYNOLDS

P. 153 THOMAS S. MAYERS APPOINTED OVERSEER IN ROOM AND STEAD OF
JOHN HANKINS

ORDERED THAT BIRD THOMAS, SHERIFF, BRING TO NEXT TERM OF COURT AN
ORPHAN BOY OF HANNAH MANOR

DANIEL J. RAWLINGS APPOINTED OVERSEER OF ROAD IN ROOM AND STEAD

OF A. J. MCCULY

PRESENT ON BENCH: SAMUEL W. ROBERSON, JONATHAN WHITESIDE,
WILLIAM BROWN, SAMUEL H. HUNTER & WILLIAM FOSTER

ISAAC B. VERNON APPEARED IN OPEN COURT, TOOK OATHS AS A JUSTICE
OF THE PEACE OF BLEDSOE COUNTY

WILLIAM FOSTER AND SAMUEL RANKIN APPOINTED TO SETTLE WITH JAMES
HOYEL, FORMER KEEPER OF THE POOR HOUSE

P. 155   ASAHEL R. THURMAN APPOINTED OVERSEER OF ROAD IN ROOM AND
STEAD OF PLEASANT VERNON...ORDERED THAT PLEASANT VERNON AND HANDS
BE ATTACHED TO THE ROAD THAT JAMES SKILLERN IS OVERSEER OF

GEORGE REAL RELEASED FROM PAYMENT OF POLE TAX FOR YEAR 1842

BURTIN LACESTER APPOINTED OVERSEER OF ROAD IN ROOM AND STEAD OF
FRANK HUGHS

BEN BROWN, DULY ELECTED CONSTABLE FOR BLEDSOE COUNTY, TOOK OATH
TO SUPPORT THE CONSTITUTION OF THE US, THE STATE OF TENNESSEE, AN
OATH AGAINST DUELLING AND OATH OF OFFICE...BOND,
$4,000.00...SECURITIES: ISAAC ROBERSON AND E. H. BOYD

FOLLOWING APPOINTED A JURY OF VIEW: D. D. CARDER, JAMES MATHISS,
JONATHAN WHITESIDE, JOHN HIXSON, S. W. ROBERSON, A. J. MCCULEY &
JOHN BRIDGMAN...TO WORK OUT A ROAD LEAVING THE TURNPIKE ROAD ON
THE SIDE OF THE MOUNTAIN...NEAR WHERE D. D. CARDER NOW LIVES,
THENCE BY OR NEAR WHERE S. W. ROBERSONS MOUNTAIN FARM IS...BY
JONATHAN WHITESIDES MOUNTAIN FARM, THEN THE MOST PRACTIABLE WAY
TO R. W. COOKES IN VAN BUREN COUNTY

P. 158   ELIZABETH PHELPS, ADMINISTRATRIX OF JOHN PHELPS,
DECEASED, RETURNED AMOUNT OF SALES OF PROPERTY OF SAID
ESTATE...ACCEPTED, ORDERED TO BE RECORDED

WILLIAM FOSTER AND SAMUEL RANKIN RETURNED REPORT OF SETTLEMENT
WITH JAMES LLOYD, FORMER TREASURY OF POOR HOUSE...INSPECTED,
ORDERED TO BE RECORDED

JESEE SHERLY APPOINTED SUPERINTENDENT OF POOR HOUSE BY
COMMISSIONERS OF THE POOR HOUSE FOR YEAR 1843...QUALIFIED,
ENTERED INTO BOND, $300.00...SECURITIES: MARTIN A SMITH AND
HENRY POLLARD

ORDERED THAT MARTIN A. SMITH, TREASURER OF POOR HOUSE PAY TO
MATTHEW PENDERGRASS $11.50

P. 161   MARCH SESSION 1843

PRESENT ON THE BENCH: S. W. ROBERSON, JONATHAN WHITESIDE,
WILLIAM BROWN, JOSEPH HIXSON, JOHN F. GREER, WILLIAM FOSTER,
ISAAC B. VERNON, GEORGE DAWSON, PHILIP S. HUTCHESON, WILLIAM
BRIANT, SAMUEL H. HUNTER, ESQS. JUSTICES & C

JURY OF VIEW: JAMES ORME, JOHN HINCH, JOHN SWAFFORD, JAMES
SWAFFORD, JAMES STEPHENS, WILLIAM KERLY, & SIMEON
SELBY...APPOINTED TO VIEW AND WORK OUT A ROAD RUNNING FROM
WILLIAM RENFRO ALL THE RITES TO MILL AND COME AND MAKE REPORT AT
APRIL TERM OF COURT

ORDERED THAT BIRD THOMAS, SHERIFF, BRING TO NEXT TERM OF COURT
THREE ORPHAN CHILDREN OF MATILDA MANING TO WIT DANIEL AND THE TWO
SMALLEST

ON APPLICATION OF ELIZABETH KIMME, WIDOW OF JOHN KIME, DECEASED,
WETHERSTON S. GREER IS APPOINTED ADMINISTRATOR OF JOHN KIMME,
DECD...QUALIFIED...BOND, $10,000.00...SECURITIES: JOHN BRIDGMAN,
JOHN F. GREER, WILLIAM RUSH, ALL OF THE COUNTY OF BLEDSOE (SEE
NAME IN NEXT ORDER.)

ISAAC STEPHENS, JAMES L. SCHOOLFIELD, & JAMES ORME APPOINTED TO
LAY OFF AND SET APART ONE YEARS PROVISION FOR THE
KIMMERS...REPORT NEXT TERM OF COURT

COURT ALLOWS THOMAS MAGERS TO OPEN A ROAD FROM CROSSVILLE SO AS
TO INTERSECT THE BRIDGE THAT WILLIAM TAUER BURITT (?BUILT) ON
OBIDS RIVER AND THAT THOMAS MAGERS KEEP UP SAID ROAD TO THE
BRIDGE

WILLIAM ROBERSON APPEARED IN COURT, TOOK OATHS AS JUSTICE OF THE
PEACE FOR BLEDSOE COUNTY

P. 165   APRIL SESSION 1843

PRESENT ON THE BENCH: ESQ. WHITESIDE, WILLIAM BROWN, RANKIN, FOSTER, GREER, ORME, PAINE, VERNON, DAWSON, S. W. ROBERSON, HUTCHESON, HIXSON, MCCLENDON, HUNTER, HERD, ISAAC RPBERSON AND BRYANT

COURT MAKE ALLOWANCE OF $4.50 TO BENJ, F. BRIDGMAN FOR RECORD BOOK

P. 166 COURT MAKES ALLOWANCE OF $19.25 TO JOHN THOMAS, CLERK, FOR FEES IN COURT

COURT MAKES ALLOWANCE TO BIRD THOMAS, SHERIFF, FOR EXIFITIO SERVICES AS SHERIFF FROM THE 4TH DAY OF AUGUST 1841 TO 3RD DAY OF APRIL 1843

JURY OF VIEW: C. C. STRANAHAN, BIRD THOMAS, E. H. BOYD, WILLIAM BROWN, S. W. ROBERSON, AND BYRAM HERD...TO VIEW AND WORK OUT AN ALTERATION IN THE ROAD LEADING ROBERT OWENS TO THE BIG ROAD SO AS TO CROSS THE BRANCH BELOW THOMPSONS...MAKE REPORT THIS TERM...THE JURY MADE FAVORABLE REPORT...ALTERATION CONFIRMED

THOMAS PRATOR APPOINTED OVERSEER OF ROAD IN THE ROOM OF JAMES SWAFFORD

ISHUM HALE APPOINTED ADMINISTRATOR OF JOHN HALE, DECEASED...APPEARED IN OPEN COURT, ENTERED INTO BOND...$500.00...SECURITIES: SARAH TERRY AND DAVID D. CARDER

COURT MADE AN APPROPRIATION OF TEN DOLLARS TO REPAIR THE BRIDGE AT PIKEVILLE...JOHN BRIDGMAN AND BIRD THOMAS APPOINTED TO SUPERINTEND THE REPAIR

COURT MADE AN APPROPRI ATION OF TEN DOLLARS TO REPAIR THE BRIDGE AT JOHN THURMANS...JOHN THURMAN AND BENJAMIN F. BRIDGMAN APPOINTED TO SUPERINTEND THE REPAIRING OF SAME

VOTE IN AFFIRMATIVE ON MAKING APPROPRIATION TO REPAIR BRIDGE AT VALENTINE SPRINGS...NO AMOUNT RECORDED...WILLIAM FOSTER AND VALENTINE SPRING APPOINTED TO SUPERINTEND REPAIRING SAME

ORDERED THAT THOMAS FOSTER, WILLIAM FOSTER VALENTINE SPRINGS AND HANDS BUILD BRIDGE AT VALENTINE SPRINGS...KEEP UP SAME

ORDERED BY THE COURT THAT TWO LINES OF DIST. NO. 1 BEE CHANGED IN
THE FOLLOWING MANNER, TO WIT BEGINNING AT CRAVEN SHERRILS OLD
PLACE AND RUNNING UP THE GRAVELY SPUR TO THE SUMMIT OF THE RIDGE
DIVIDING THE WATER OF THE GRASSY COVE AND SODDY CREEKINCLUDING
WILLIAM HOLOWAYS IN DIST. NO. 2 THENCE WITH SAID RIDGE INCLUDING
JAMES HEDGECOTH IN THE 1ST DIST. TO THE STAGE ROAD NEAR HIRAM
HEDGECOTHS THENCE A DIRECT LINE TO THE RHEA COUNTY LINE ALSO
ANOTHER LINE COMMENCING AT SAID SHERILS RUNNING A DIRECT LINE TO
THE FORKS OF DADYS CREEK AND LICK CREEK THENCE UP LICK CREEK TO
THE ROAD LEADING FROM CHARLES LOWERYS TO THE SEQUATCHY VALY
INCLUDING JOHN WAITS THENCE TO THE HEAD OF A BRANCH THE WATERS OF
BIG LAUREL WHERE REBECCA HINES LIVES THENCE WITH SAID BRANCH
INCLUDING WILLIAM K. WILTTS TO THE WHITE COUNTY LINE

WILLIAM WALKER, COUNTY TRUSTEE, ALLOWED SIX DOLLARS EIGHTY-SEVEN
AND A HALF CENTS FOR MONIES ALLOWED TO JOHN BILLINGSLY STRAYS
PROVEN AWAY & C

SAMUEL W. ROBERSON APPOINTED GUARDIAN OF MINOR HEIRS OF NANCY
HAY...CAME INTO COURT, QUALIFIED...BOND, $50.00...SECURITIES:
WM. FOSTER AND ISAAC ROBERSON

P. 174 ALLOWANCE OF FIVE DOLLARS EACH TO REVINUE COMMISSIONERS:
GEORGE DAWSON, JOHN F. GREER, JAMES ORME, WILLIAM BROWN, SAMUEL
RANKIN, SAMUEL W. ROBERSON, WILLIAM FOSTER, WILLIAM BRIANT,
JOSEPH HIXSON, AND BYRAM HERD

WETHERSTON S. GREER, ADMINISTRATOR OF ESTATE OF JOHN KIMMER,
DECD, RETURNED INVENTORY AND AMOUNT OF ESTATE...INSPECTED BY
COURT, ORDERED TO RECORD

COURT APPOINTS ROBERT DWIGGINS TAX COLLECTOR FOR YEAR
1843...QUALIFIED...ENTERED INTO BOND...$2,000.00...SECURITIES:
JAMES L. SCHOOLFIELD AND JEREMIAH DORSEY.....ANOTHER BOND,
$10,000.00...SECURITIES: JAMES L. SCHOOLFIELD AND SAMUEL RANKIN

COMMISSIONER APPOINTED AT MARCH TERM TO LAY OFF AND SET APART ONE
YEARS PROVISION FOR THE WIDOW OF JOHN KIMMER, DECEASED RETURNED
FOLLOWING REPORT:
1200 LBS BACON & 10 CHOICE HOGS
400 BUSHELS CORN NOW 400 IN FULL
200 LBS COFFEE
200 LBS SUGAR
800 LBS FLOWER
20 DOLLARS FOR LEATHER
12 DOLLARS FOR SHEWMAKING
2 BLLS. SALT
200 LBS HOG LARD AND ALL SOAP AND LARD ON HAND

40 LBS COTTON   40 LBS WOOL
50 LBS TALLOW
10 DOLLARS FOR NECESSARIES AND THE USE OF 4 MILK COWS ONE YEAR
ALL THE HAY AND FODDER ON THE PLACE, THERE NOT BEING MORE THAN A
SUFFICIENCY ONE BEEF STEW ON HAND 20 BUSHELS OATS

ON APPLICATION OF WETHERSTON S. GREER, JAMES L. SCHOOLFIELD
APPOINTED GUARDIAN OF MINOR HEIRS OF JOHN KIMMER,
DECEASED...BOND...$10,000.00...SECURITIES: BIRD THOMAS, ROBERT
DWIGGINS, WETHERSTON S. GREER...CHILDREN: ELIZA, MORGAN,
CHRISTOPHER, ANDREW, SARAH

ON APPLICATION OF JOHN THOMAS, CLERK, WETHERSTON S. GREER
APPEARED IN COURT, QUALIFIED TO PERFORM DUTIES OF DEPUTY CLERK

ORDERED THAT THE SHERIFF BRING TO NEXT TERM OF COURT TWO CHILDREN
OF JULIAN FOSTER TO BE DISPOSED OF AS THE COURT MAY THINK PROPER

JURY OF VIEW: JOHNATHAN WHITESIDE, JOHN BRIDGEMAN, BIRD THOMAS,
WILLIAM BROWN, JAMES SPARKS, AND SAMUEL W. ROBERSON...TO VIEW AND
MARK OUT A ROAD LEADING FROM THE VALY ROAD NEAR HENSONS UP THE
MOUNTAIN AT THE HENSON GAP AND THENCE THE NEXT PROACHABLE WAY TO
S. W. ROBERSON FROM THENCE BY OR NEAR PENDERGRASS DWELLING AND
THENCE BY JONATHAN WHITESIDE MOUNTAIN FARM FROM THENCE A DIRECT
COURSE TO R. W. COOK IN VANBUREAN COUNTY...REPORT AT MAY TERM

ORDERED THAT FOLLOWING GENTLEMEN BE SUMMONED TO ATTEND AS JURORS
AT JULY TERM OF THE CIRCUIT COURT FOR BLEDSOE COUNTY 1843:
GEORGE DAWSON   ISAAC B. VERNON
JOSEPH B. MCCLENDON   THOMAS FOSTER
JAMES WALKER   PRESTON MCCLENDON
WILLIAM LADEN   OBIDIAH WRIGHT
WILLIAM PAYNE   ARON HUGHS
JOSEPH PATTON   RIGHT JOHNSON
JOSEPH MCDOWEL   JOSEPH J. HOGE
JESSEE C. BROWN   ALEXANDER POPE
JOHN W. ACUFF   E. H. BOYD
WILLIAM THOMAS   JAMES LLOYD
JOHN BRIDGMAN
WILLIAM S. DALTON
JAMES SKILLERN
SAMUEL VERNON

AND THAT BEN A. BROWN & ROBERT DWIGGINS BE SUMMONED TO WAIT ON
THE COURT

P. 181 JOHN LEE APPOINTED OVERSEER IN ROOM AND STEAD OF JAMES A.
THURMAN...SAID LEE TO HAVE CALVIN AND MILTON FERGUSON EXTRA OF

ALLOWANCE OF $30.00 TO JOSEPH C. NEWMAN FOR SIX MONTHS, TO BE
PAID QUARTERLY...JAMES ORME TO DRAW THE MONEY AND TO APPLY IT TO
SAID NEWMAN USE

P. 183

THE STATE   )
   VS   )
PETER HOODENPYL   )   BASTARDY

ORDERED BY THE COURT THAT THE DEFENDANT PETER HOODENPYL PAY TO
ANNA ROGERS THE SUM OF TWENTY DOLLARS FOR THE FIRST YEAR. TEN
DOLLARS FOR THE SECOND YEAR AND FIVE DOLLARS FOR THE THIRD YEAR,
TO BE PAID QUARTERLY FROM THE 3RD DAY OF APRIL 1843...THEREUPON,
PETER HOODENPYL MADE BOND, $100.00, SECURITIES JAMES A. TULLOSS
AND BIRD THOMAS...HAS BEEN CONVICTED OF GETTING A BASTARD CHILD
OF THE BODY OF ANNA ROGERS

P. 184   MAY SESSION   1843

PRESENT ON THE BENCH: ESQ. JONATHAN WHITESIDE, COL. BROWN, JAMES
ORME, JOSEPH HIXSON

WILLIAM KERLEY, GUARDIAN OF MINOR HEIRS OF DANIEL KERLY,
DECEASED, RETURNED INTO COURT A SETTLEMENT WHICH WAS INSPECTERD,
ORDERED TO RECORD

JOHN THOMAS RETURNED INTO COURT A SETTLEMENT MADE WITH WILLIAM
WALKER, COUNTY TRUSTEE SHOWING THE DISBURSEMENTS OF COMMON SCHOOL
FUND FOR YEAR 1842...ORDERED TO RECORD

ISUM HALE RETURNED INVENTORY OF THE AMOUNT OF ESTATE OF JOHN HALE
DSD...INSPECTED, ORDERED TO RECORD

P. 185   JONATHAN WHITESIDE, ET AL, JURY OF VIEW, ALLOWED UNTIL
NEXT TERM TO MAKE REPORT

JAMES ORME APPOINTED GUARDIAN OF MINOR HEIRS OF AMY LOWE, DAVID
AND JAMES LOWE...QUALIFIED, ENTERED INTO
BOND...$250.00...SECURITIES: SAMUEL RANKIN AND SAMUEL OXSHER

SAMUEL H. HUNTER, JACOB TETERS & BYRAM HERD APPOINTED TO LAY OFFAND SET APART ONE YEARS PROVISION FOR THE WIDOW OF JOHN HALE, DECEASED...REPORT NEXT TERM

JUNE SESSION 1843

P. 190 PRESENT ON THE BENCH: JONATHAN WHITESIDE, HUNTER, RANKIN, FOSTER, BROWN, BRIANT, GIPSON, SMITH

JAMES A. WHITESIDE APPOINTED ADMINISTRATOR OF ESTATE OF PLUNKETT F. GLENTWORTH, DECD, LATE A CITIZEN OF NEW JERSEY...OWNED PERSONAL PROPERTY IN THIS COUNTY AT TIME OF HIS DEATH...WHITESIDE QUALIFIED...BOND, $2,000.00...SECURITIES: JONATHAN WHITESIDE AND JAMES L. SCHOOLFIELD

EDWIN BAITY APPOINTED OVERSEER OF ROAD IN ROOM AND STEAD OF JOHN GENTRY

P. 190 ORDERED THAT ANDERSON ONEIL AN ORPHAN BOY BE BOUND TO JOHN THURMAN UNTILL HE ARRIVES TO THE AGE OF TWENTY-ONE YEARS...BOND AND AGREEMENT...JAMES HIXSON, SECURITY

W. HENDERSON APPOINTED OVERSEER OF ROAD IN ROOM OF ISAAC N. BUSELL

BYRAM HERD, JACOB TETERS & SAMUEL H. HUNTER RETURNED INTO COURT REPORT ONE YEARS PROVISION FOR THE WIDOW OF JOHN HALE, DECD...INSPECTED, ORDERED TO RECORD

JOHN DAY PRODUCED ONE WOLF SCALP...SWORN...WOLF WAS OVER FOUR MONTHS OLD...CERTIFICATE ISSUED

ISUM HALE, ADMINISTRATOR OF JOHN HALE, DECD. RETURNED INVENTORY AND AMOUNT OF SALES OF PROPERTY OF JOHN HALE, DECD...INSPECTED, ORDERED TO RECORD

P. 192 MARTIN A. SMITH COMMISSIONED JUSTICE OF THE PEACE FOR BLEDSOE COUNTY...TOOK OATHS

WETHERSTON S. GREER, ADMINISTRATOR OF ESTATE OF JOHN KIMMER, DECD RETURNED AMOUNT OF SALES OF SAID ESTATE...INSPECTED, ORDERED TO RECORD

JURY OF VIEW: THOMAS GREEN, WILLIAM THOMAS, JOHN H. ACUFF,
MORGAN GREEN, AND ISAAC S. ANDERSON...TO VIEW AND MARK OUT A ROAD
COMMENCING AT THE MOUTH OF THE LANE BETWEEN JOHN HUTCHESONS AND
AQUILLA JOHNSON RUNNING ACROSS THE VALY SO AS TO INTERSECT THE
MAIN VALY ROAD AT OR NEAR J. DORSEY AT THE OLD HUNTER
TRACT...REPORT NEXT TERM

P. 193 ORDERED THAT ALL HANDS IN THE FOLLOWING BOUNDS WORK UNDER
ELLIOTT H. BOYD AS OVERSEER, TO WIT: COMMENCING AT THE HEAD OF
ALEXANDER LAMBS SPRING BRANCH, THENCE WITH SAID BRANCH UNTILL IT
INTERSECTS SEQUATCHY RIVER, THENCE UP SAID RIVER TO THE FORD
WHERE REEL NOW LIVES, THENCE A DIRECT CORSE TO THE LOWER CORNER
OF WILLIAM BRIANTS FIELD ON THE STAGE ROAD, THENCE DIRECT TO THE
SIDE OF THE MOUNTAIN, INCLUDING ALL THE HANDS IN SAID BOUNDRY SO
AS NOT TO INTERFERE WITH THOSE THAT WORK ON ROBERSON CROSS ROAD

A. H. COULTER APPOINTED OVERSEER OF ROAD IN ROOM AND STEAD OF
BURTON LACESETER

HARDY COX RELEASED FROM PAYMENT OF POLE TAX FOR THE YEAR 1841 &
1842

P. 194   JULY   SESSION   1843

PRESENT ON THE BENCH: JONATHAN WHITESIDE, SAMUEL W. ROBERSON,
WILLIAM BROWN, WILLIAM FOSTER, SAMUEL H. HUNTER, WILLIAM BRIANT,
SAMUEL RANKIN, ISAAC ROBERSON

THOMAS MAUSSE APPOINTED ADMINISTRATOR OF ESTATE OF ROBERT FERR,
DECD...ENTERED INTO BOND...$800.00...SECURITIES: A. H. COULTER &
JAMES HENSON...S/THOMAS MAUSY

WILIE REDWINE RELEASED FROM PAYMENT OF A POLE TAX FOR YEAR 1842

JOHN THOMAS, CLERK, PRODUCED SETTLEMENT MADE WITH JOHN TOLLETT,
ADMINISTRATOR OF WILSON TOLLETT, DECD...INSPECTED, ORDERED TO
RECORD

GREEN J. SHELBY HAS BEEN ELECTED CONSTABLE FOR BLEDSOE
COUNTY...QUALIFIED, ENTERED INTO BOND...SECURITIES: JAMES ORME
AND JOHN TOLLETT

JOHN THOMAS PRODUCED SETTLEMENT MADE WITH WILLIAM FOSTER,

GUARDIAN OF MINOR HEIRS OF DAVID PAINE...INSPECTED, ORDERED TO
RECORD

WILLIAM KEEDY APPOINTED OVERSEER OF ROAD IN ROOM AND STEAD OF
HUGH PIKE

JOHN O. THOMPSON, ELECTED CONSTABLE FOR BLEDSOE COUNTY...ENTERED
INTO BOND...$4,000.00...SECURITIES: GEORGE DAWSON AND JOHN F.
GREER

COURT ELECTED SURVEYOR FOR BLEDSOE COUNTY: PETER HOODENPYL

LEVI CARTER ALLOWED $17.00 FOR KEEPING A PAUPER FROM THE 3RD DAY
OF JULY 1843

ORDERED THAT THE ROAD LEADING FROM HUGH BAITYS TO THE BIG SPRING
BE DIVIDED...CREEK, THE LINE...HENRY CLOSE APPOINTED OVERSEER OF
THE EAST END...JOEL SEGRAVES APPOINTED OVERSEER OF THE WEST END

WILLIAM WALKER, COUNTY TRUSTEE, GAVE BOND FOR RECEIVING AND
DISBURSING THE COMMON SCHOOL FUND FOR
1843...$10,000.00...SECURITIES: WILLIAM FOSTER AND A. H. COULTER

A. H. COULTER APPOINTED OVERSEER OF ROAD COMMENCING AT MAY JOSEPH
HIXSONS BRANCH AND RUNNING UP TO THE CROSS ROAD WHERE GEORGE REEL
NOW LIVES...HAVE ALL HANDS IN THAT BOUND ON EAST SIDE OF RIVER

ALLOWANCE TO A. H. MONTGOMERY...$4.62 1/2 CENTS

P. 203 ALLOWANCE TO ELISHA KIRKLIN...$3.60 FOR AND OVER
REALIZATION OF HIS PROPERTY

WILLIAM FOSTER RELEASED FROM PAYMENT OF POLE TAX FOR THE YEAR
1842 AND 1843

ORDERED THAT THE SHERIFF SUMMONS THE FOLLOWING GENTLEMEN TO
ATTEND AS JUDGES AT THE ENSUING AUGUST ELECTION:
  1. JOHN NARRAMORE, SAMUEL MILLER, HIRAM HEDGCOTH
  2. WILLIAM GIPSON, W. S. GREER, JOHN FORD
  3. WILLIAM NAIL, JOHN TOLLETT, ISAAC STEPHENS
  4. WILLIAM MCDOWEL, J. G. M. WOODS, ROBERT WRIGHT
  5. JOHN BILLINGSLEY, RICHARD GREEN, I. L. ANDERSON
  6. JOHN THURMAN, WM. STEPHENS, BIRD HENSON

7. LEWIS KEEDY, VALENTINE SPRING, THOMAS SUTHERLAND
8. WILLIAM WALKER, ISAAC ROBERSON, OBIDIAH RIGHT
9. JOHN B. CROZIER, HARDY LACESETER, RIGHT JOHNSON
10. JAMES NICHOLS, J. B. WHEELER, T. J. POPE

P. 205 PETER HOODENPYL APPEARED IN OPEN COURT...QUALIFIED AS
SURVEYOR OF BLEDSOE COUNTY...ENTERED INTO
BOND...$25,000.00...SECURITIES: BIRD THOMAS AND WILLIAM WALKER

P. 207 AUGUST SESSION 1843

PRESENT ON THE BENCH: SAMUEL W. ROBERSON, JONATHAN WHITESIDE,
WILLIAM BROWN

JAMES A. TULLOSS, FORMER CLERK OF BLEDSOE COUNTY, PRODUCED A
RECEIPT FOR STATE REVENUE DUE FROM THE 1ST SEPT 1841 TO 4TH APRIL
1842...$147.44

P. 208 JOHN THOMAS, CLERK, PRODUCED SETTLEMENT MADE WITH MARY
MASSEE, GUARDIAN OF MINOR HEIRS OF RICHARD MASSEE,
DECD...INSPECTED, ORDERED TO RECORD

J. B. WHEELER APPOINTED OVERSEER OF ROAD IN ROOM OF JOHN
JOHNSON...BENJAMIN BRIANT APPOINTED IN STEAD OF WILLIAM ROGERS

ANNA COOK APPOINTED ADMINISTRATOR OF ESTATE OF WILLIAM B. COOK,
DECEASED...ENTERED INTO BOND, $500.00...SECURITIES THOMAS FARMER,
DAVID D. CARDER, BIRD THOMAS

JAMES R. BROWN APPOINTED OVERSEER OF ROAD IN ROOM OF HEZEKIAH
KERTIS

THOMAS MAUGE, ADMINISTRATOR OF ESTATE OF ROBERT FARE, DECD,
RETURNED INVENTORY OF PROPERTY BELONGING TO ESTATE...INSPECTED,
ORDERED TO RECORD

P. 211 ANNA COOK, ADMINISTRATRIX OF ESTATE OF WILLIAM R. COOK,
DECD, RETURNED INVENTORY OF PROPERTY OF SAID ESTATE...INSPECTED,
ORDERED TO RECORD

BURTON LACESETER, ELECTED CONSTABLE FOR BLEDSOE COUNTY,
QUALIFIED...BOND, $4,000.00...SECURITIES: HARDY LACESETER AND
JAMES LACESETER

P. 213 ORDERED THAT THE SHERIFF SUMMONS THE FOLLOWING GENTLEMEN
TO ATTEND AS JURORS AT THE NOVEMBER TERM OF CIRCUIT COURT
FORBLEDSOE COUNTY FOR THE YEAR 1843: CHARLES LOWERY, GEORGE
DAWSON, JOHN F. GREER, WETHERSTON S. GREER, JAMES ORME, JAMES L.
SCHOOLFIELD, BURELL LEE, J. G. M. WOODS, ROBERT WORTHINGTON, WM.
BROWN, JAMES MARTIN A. SMITH, F. A. JOHNSON, JONATHAN WHITESIDE,
PLEASANT VERNON, SAMUEL MCREYNOLDS, SAMUEL W. ROBERSON, LEWIS
KEEDY JR., JOHN LEE, OBIDIAH RIGHT, WILLIAM HASKEW, JESSEE
COLBERT, JOSEPH HIXSON, HENRY HORN, BYRAM HERD, WILLIAM HUNTER
...JONATHAN ACUFF AND   M. ANDERSON BE SUMMONED TO WAIT ON COURT

WILLIAM VERNON, MARTIN A. SMITH AND WILLIAM STEPHENS APPOINTED TO
LAY OFF AND SET APART ONE YEARS PROVISION FOR THE WIDOW OF WILLIAM
R. COOK...REPORT NEXT TERM

ORDERED THAT THE ORDER MADE AT APRIL TERM APPOINTING ROBERT
DWIGGINS TAX COLLECTOR FOR YEAR 1843 BE RECEIVED

P. 214   SEPTEMBER SESSION   1843

PRESENT ON THE BENCH: JONAATHAN WHITESIDE, WILLIAM BROWN, S. W.
ROBERSON, WILLIAM FOSTER, SAMUEL H. HUNTER

WILLIAM RECTOR APPOINTED OVERSEER OF ROAD IN ROOM AND STEAD OF
JESSEE BROWN...RIGHT JOHNSON APPOINTED IN STEAD OF ARON
HICKENBOTTOM

P. 215 ANNA COOK, ADMINISTRATRIX OF ESTATE OF WILLIAM R. COOK
RETURNED AMOUNT OF SALES OF PROPERTY OF SAID ESTATE...INSPECTED,
ORDERED TO RECORD

SAMUEL C. WHITE APPOINTED OVERSEER OF ROAD IN STEAD OF JOHN D.
MORRIS

JAMES COWAN RELEASED FROM PAYMENT OF A POLE TAX FOR YEAR 1843

THOMAS MAUGE, ADMINISTRATOR OF ESTATE OF ROBERT FARR, DECD,
RETURNED AMOUNT OF SALES OF SAID ESTATE...INSPECTED, ORDERED TO
RECORD

JOHN THOMAS, CLERK, PRODUCED IN OPEN COURT A RECEIPT FROM WILLIAM
WALKER, COUNTY TRUSTEE FOR REVINUE COLLECTED AS SUCH
CLERK...$31.68 AND 3/4 CENTS

P. 216 CATHARINE THOMAS CAME INTO OPEN COURT AND PROVED
DECLARATION FOR A PENSION AS THE WIDOW OF JOHN THOMAS, DECEASED
WHO WAS A SOLDIER OF THE REVOLUTION...APPROVED BY THE COURT

KESIAH THURMAN CAME INTO OPEN COURT AND PROVED A DECLARATION FOR
A PENSION AS THE WIDOW OF PHILIP THURMAN, DECEASED WHO WAS A
SOLDIER OF THE REVOLUTION...SAME APPROVED BY COURT

WILLIAM L. DALTON, ENTERTAKER OF BLEDSOE COUNTY APPROVED IN OPEN
COURT AND DISMISSED BIRD PANKEY WHO HAD BEEN FORMERLY DEPUTY
ENTERTAKER AND APPOINTED THOMAS R. ROGERS HIS DEPUTY...ROGERS
APPEARED IN OPEN COURT AND QUALIFIED AS SUCH

ON APPLICATION OF JOHN THOMAS, CLERK, JAMES A. TULLOSS APPEARED
IN OPEN COURT AND WAS QUALIFIED TO PERFORM DUTIES OF DEPUTY CLERK

P. 217 OCTOBER SESSION 1843

PRESENT ON THE BENCH: THE WORSHIPFUL JAMES ORME, SAMUEL H.
HUNTER, SAMUEL W. ROBERSON, JONATHAN WHITESIDE, WILLIAM BROWN,
WILLIAM PAYNE, D. S. HUTCHESON, ISAAC ROBERSON, WILLIAM FOSTER,
M. A. SMITH

JOHN STUBS APPOINTED OVERSEER OF ROAD IN ROOM AND STEAD OF
HENDERSON CONLY

REPORT OF COMMISSIONER APPOINTED AT LAST TERM TO SET APART
PROVISIONS FOR AMY COOK, WIDOW AND RELICT OF W. R. COOK: 150
BUSHELS OF CORN OUT OF PRESENT CROP, GIVING SIX OF THE BEST HOGS,
AND TWENTY DOLLARS OUT OF MONEY BELONGING TO SAID ESTATE...REPORT
CONFIRMED

JOHN LEA APPOINTED AS OVERSEER OF ROAD IN ROOM OF THOS. SWAFFORD

A. H. COULTER, CORONER OF BLEDSOE COUNTY, ALLOWED SUM OF FIVE
DOLLARS...FOR HOLDING AN INQUEST OVER THE BODY OF A BOY CHILD ON
THE 5TH DAY OF AUGUST 1843

SAMUEL C. WHITE APPOINTED OVERSEER OF ROAD IN ROOM OF JOHN D.
MORRIS

P. 219 JURY OF VIEW: ROBERT WORTHINGTON SEN., GEORGE F. JONES,
BENJAMIN HAMILTON, JAMES L. SCHOOLFIELD, THOMAS HALE, JAMES

WALKER AND JOHN SWAFFORD (CURLY HEAD)...TO VIEW AND MARK OUT A PUBLIC ROAD OF SECOND CLASS TO COMMENCE AT OR NEAR WHERE THE VALY ROAD CROSSES ISAAC STEVENS SPRING BRANCH, THENCE UP CUMBERLAND MOUNTAIN, THENCE THE NEAREST AND BEST WAY TO INTERSECT THE MAIN SURVEY ROAD ON THE TOP OF A RISE BEYOND JOHN WYATTS...MAKE REPORT AT JANUARY TERM

JURY OF VIEW: JOSEPHMCDOWELL, WILLIAM MCDOWELL, THOMAS SMITH, JOHN BILLINGSLEY, THOS. SWAFFORD, AND ROBERT WORTHINGTON JR...TO VIEW AND MAKE ALTERATION IN PUBLIC ROAD COMMENCING AT WILLIAM WORTHINGTON SO AS TO RUN UP BEATTES MILL BRANCH INSTEAD OF WHERE IT RUNS AT THIS TIME...REPORT AT JANY TERM

P. 220 JURY OF VIEW: AARON HUGHES, HENRY HORN, JOHN HUGHS, FRANK HUGHS, A. H. COULTER, HARDY LASETER AND GEORGE H. BILLINGSLEY...TO VIEW AND MAKE ALTERATION IN PUBLIC ROAD COMMENCING AT HENRY HORNS TO INTERSECT THE OLD ROAD AT OR NEAR JOHN GRAHAMS...REPORT AT JANY TERM

JURY OF VIEW: B. F. BRIDGMAN, JAMES LLOYD, JOHN THURMAN, JOHN SKILLERN, JAMES SKILLERN, JONATHAN WHITESIDE, AND PLEASANT VERNON...TO VIEW AND MARK OUT A PUBLIC ROAD COMMENCING AT OR NEAR B. F. BRIDGMANS, THENCE RUNNING BY QUARLES MILL, THENCE UP THE MOUNTAINTO A CABIN BUILT BY DANIEL QUARLES ON THE TURNPIKE ROAD, THENCE IN THE DIRECTION TO HENRY MILLERS OLD PLACE NEAR THE COUNTY LINE BETWEEN BLEDSOE AND RHEA COUNTIES...REPORT JANY TERM

P. 221 WILLIAM FOSTER APPOINTED TRUSTEE OF THE LAFAYETTE ACADEMY IN TOWN OF PIKEVILLE IN THE PLACE AND STEAD OF JONATHAN WHITESIDE RESIGNED

THOMAS GRAHAM APPOINTED OVERSEER OF ROAD IN ROOM AND STEAD OF E. H. BOYD...ALLEN MERRIMAN APPOINTED OVERSEER IN ROOM OF ABLE HARRISON

BIRD THOMAS, SHERIFF, CAME INTO COURT AND ENTERED INTO BOND FOR HIS FAITHFULLY COLLECTING AND ACCOUNTING FOR THE REVENUE OF BLEDSOE COUNTY DUE THE STATE AND COUNTY FOR YEAR 1843...BOND, $10,000.00...SECURITIES, JAMES ORME AND PETER HOODENPYLE...ANOTHER BOND FOR $2,000.00, SAME SECURITIES

P. 224 HUGH PIKE APPOINTED OVERSEER OF ROAD IN ROOM AND STEAD OF VALENTINE SPRING...TO HAVE THE FOLLOWING HANDS: GEORGE OXSHER, MARK PIKE, O. C. BEACH, SAMON BEACH, WYATT M. HUMBLE AND WILEY HAMBLE

ORDER MADE AT LAST TERM OF COURT APPOINTING JOHN LOWERY OVERSEER
OF PUBLIC ROAD RESINDED AND HELD TO BE VOID...ARON SWAFFORD IS
HEREBY APPOINTED IN THE ROOM AND STEAD

ROBERT DWIGGINS TENDERED HIS RESIGNATION AS CONSTABLE...RECEIVED
BY COURT

ORDERED THAT SHERIFF BRING TO NEXT TERM OF COURT TWO CHILDREN OF
TWELVE ANN FOSTERS TO BE DEALT WITH AS THE COURT THINKS PROPER

P. 225 SAMUEL OXSHER CAME INTO COURT AND RESIGNED FROM BEING
DEPUTY SHERIFF ANY LONGER

BIRD THOMAS, SHERIFF, APPOINTED ROBERT DWIGGINS DEPUTY...DWIGGINS
APPEARD, TOOK OATH

P. 226 NOVEMBER SESSION 1843

PRESENT ON THE BENCH: THE WORSHIPFUL WHITESIDE, S. W. ROBERSON,
ISAAC ROBERSON, FOSTER, COL. BROWN & M. A. SMITH

GEORGE FINLEY APPOINTED OVERSEER OF ROAD IN ROOM AND STEAD OF
JOEL HALE

JOHN THOMAS, CLERK, PRODUCED SETTLEMENT MADE WITH MAY CLARK,
GUARDIAN OF MINOR HEIRS OF JOHN CLARK, DECEASED...INSPECTED,
ORDERED TO RECORD

JOHN M. BILLINGSLEY APPOINTED OVERSEER OF ROAD IN ROOM AND STEAD
OF JAMES BILLINGSLEY

ENOCH WILOUGHBY, DULY ELECTED AS CONSTABLE FOR BLEDSOE, APPEARED
IN COURT, TOOK OATHS...ENTERED INTO BOND, $4,000.00...SECURITIES,
SAMUEL RANKIN, AND THOMAS S. MOYSES

WALTER T. GREER PRODUCED IN OPEN COURT ONE WOLF SCALP...WOLF WAS
OVER FOUR MONTHS OLD...CERTIFICATE ISSUED

S. W. ROBERSON RESIGNED AS QUORAM COURT AND WILLIAM FOSTER WAS
ELECTED TO FILL THE VACANCY

P. 228 KESIAH THURMAN WIDOW OF PHILIP THURMAN DESD, APPEARED IN
OPEN COURT AND PROVED A DECLARATION THAT SHE IS THE WIFE OF SAID
PHILIP THURMAN, DECEASED

COURT ORDERED SHERIFF BRING TO NEXT TERM OF COURT TWO CHILDREN OF
JULIAN FOSTERS TO BE DEALT WITH AS THE COURT MAY THINK PROPER

P. 230   DECEMBER SESSION 1843

PRESENT ON THE BENCH: THE WORSHIPFUL WHITESIDE, WILLIAM FOSTER,
AND WILLIAM BROWN

JOHN THOMAS, CLERK, PRODUCED IN COURT A SETTLEMENT MADE WITH
JOSEPH HIXSON, GUARDIAN OF MINOR HEIRS OF JOHN HIXSON,
DECEASED...INSPECTED, ORDERED TO RECORD

JOHN THOMAS, CLERK, PRODUCED A SETTLEMENT MADE WITH JANE ROGERS,
GUARDIAN OF MINOR HEIRS OF FREDERICK J. ROGERS, DESD...APPROVED,
ORDERED TO RECORD

JOHN THOMAS, CLERK, PRODUCED IN OPEN COURT SETTLEMENT WITH
WILLIAM BROWN, GUARDIAN OF MINOR HEIRS OF JOSIAH CRAWFORD,
DESD...INSPECTED, ORDERED TO RECORD

P. 231   ORDERED THAT THE FOLLOWING GENTLEMEN BE APPOINTED
REVENUE COMMISSIONERS FOR THE YEAR 1844:   JOSEPH B. MCCLENDEN,
WILLIAM GIPSON, JAMES ORME, PHILIP HUTCHESON, M. A. SMITH,
JONATHAN WHITESIDE, WM. FOSTER, ISAAC ROBERSON, SAMUEL H. HUNTER,
JOEL WHEELER

ORDERED THAT SHERIFF SUMMONS FOLLOWING GENTLEMEN TO ATTEND AS
JURORS AT THE MARCH TERM OF THE CIRCUIT COURT FOR BLEDSOE COUNTY
FOR THE YEAR 1844:   CHARLES LOWRY, JOHN STUBS, WETHERSTON S.
GREER, NATHANIEL BRISTOL, JAMES L. SCHOOLFIELD, JAMES RECTOR,
ROBERT WORTHINGTON, PHILIP S. HUTCHESON, WILLIAM WORTHINGTON,
WILLIAM BROWN, SAMUEL RANKIN, WILLIAM FANN, ISAAC S. ANDERSON, B.
F. BRIDGMAN, JOHN BRIDGMAN, E. M. HALE, JAMES LLOYD, C. C.
STRANAHAN, E. H. BOYD, WILLIAM BRIANT, WILLIAM L. BROWN, JAMES
LACESETER, HARDY LACESETER, ROBERT OWENS, E. M. EVANS, AND THAT
JAMES T. NANNY AND D. D. CARDER BE SUMMONED TO WAIT ON SAID COURT

WILLIAM L. BROWN APPEARED IN OPEN COURT AND RESIGNED AS GUARDIAN
OF THE MINOR HEIRS OF JOSIAH CRAWFORD, DECEASED

JOHN THOMAS, CLERK, PRODUCED IN OPEN COURT A SETTLEMENT MADE WITH
BYRAM HERD, ADMINISTRATOR OF DAVID SMITH, DESD...INSPECTED,
ORDERED TO RECORD

JOHN THOMAS, CLERK, PRODUCED IN OPEN COURT A SETTLEMENT MADE WITH
WILLIAM KERLEY, GUARDIAN OF MINOR HEIRS OF DANIEL KERLY,
DECEASED...INSPECTED BY COURT, ORDERED TO RECORD

JURY OF VIEW: J. H. ACUFF, MORGAN GREEN, THOMAS GREEN, A. B.
CARNES, JOHN M. BILLINGSLEY, NICHOLAS ACUFF, & AMOS
SIMMONS...APPOINTED TO VIEW AND MARK OUT A ROAD OF THIRD CLASS
COMMENCING AT JOHN HUTCHESONS AND RUNNING ACROSS THE RIVER TO
INTERSECT THE VALLY ROAD AT OR NEAR J. DORSEYS...MAKE REPORT NEXT
TERM

THOMAS R. ROGERS APPEARED IN OPEN COURT...QUALIFIED AS DEPUTY
REGISTER FOR BLEDSOE COUNTY

MARTIN A. SMITH APPEARED IN OPEN COURT AND WAS APPOINTED GUARDIAN
OF MINOR HEIRS OF JOSIAH CRAWFORD, DESD...ENTERED BOND, $624.00,
SECURITIES, WILLIAM L. BROWN AND A. M. ANDERSON

P. 235 JANUARY SESSION 1844   JAN. 1, 1844

PRESENT ON BENCH: THE WORSHIPFUL JONATHAN WHITESIDE, WILLIAM
FOSTER, SAMUEL H. HUNTER, WILLIAM BRIANT, JOSEPH HIXSON, ISAAC
ROBERSON, PHILIP S. HUTCHESON, SAMUEL RANKIN, MARTIN A. SMITH,
WILLIAM BROWN, JAMES ORME, WILLIAM GIPSON, ELISHA KIRKLIN, BYRAM
HERD & JOEL WHEELER ESQ.

JAMES ORME, MARTIN A. SMITH & WILLIAM BROWN APPOINTED TO
SUPERINTEND THE POOR HOUSE FOR THE YEAR 1844...MARTIN A. SMITH
APPOINTED TREASURER OF POOR HOUSE, ENTERED INTO BOND,
$200.00...SECURITY: WILLIAM WORTHINGTON

ALLOWANCE OF TEN DOLLARS TO MARTIN A. SMITH, TREASURER OF THE
POOR HOUSE AND FIVE DOLLARS EACH TO WILLIAM BROWN AND JAMES ORME,
SUPERINTENDENT OF POOR HOUSE

P. 237 COURT ELECTED WILLIAM BROWN CHAIRMAN OF COURT FOR YEAR
1844

ALLOWANCE OF ONE DOLLAR EACH TO KORUM COURT THAT SERVED , 1843

COURT PROCEEDED TO ELECT A COURT QUORUM FOR YEAR 1844:   JO ATHAN
WHITESIDE, JAMES ORME AND SAMUEL RANKIN

SAMUEL W. ROBERSON APPOINTED OVERSEER OF ROAD IN ROOM AND STEAD
OF ROBERT OWENS

P. 238   JOSEPH PATTON APPOINTED OVERSEER IN ROOM OF JOHN
HINCH...JACK TOLLETT APPOINTED IN ROOM OF WILSON TOLLETT,
DECEASED

REPORT OF ROBERT WORTHINGTON, ET AL, JURY OF VIEW: PERFORMED THE
DUTY AS SIGNED THEM...DO AGREE...SAID ROAD SHALL BEGIN WHERE
ISAAC STEPHENS SPRING BRANCH CROSSES THE SAME, THENCE BY SAID
STEPHENS DWELLING HOUSE, THENCE BY BENNETT RECTORS, THENCE
FOLLOWING THE DUG ROAD TO THE TOP OF THE MOUNTAIN, THENCE TO THE
TOP OF THE HILL BEYOND JOHN WIATTS TO INTERSECT LOWERYS ROAD
...ORDERED BY COURT THAT ABOVE ROAD BE ESTABLISHED...JAMES WALKER
APPOINTED OVERSEER, AND HAVE THE HANDS IN THE FOLLOWING BOUNDS:
BEGINNING AT THE PUBLIC ROAD WHERE JAMES STEPHENS SPRING BRANCH
CROSSES THE SAME, UP SAID BRANCH TO THE MOUTH OF WILLIAM KERLEYS
BRANCH, THENCE TO GEORGE PRESLEYS, THENCE TO THE TOP OF
CUMBERLAND MOUNTAINTO THE LOWERY ROAD, THENCE ALONG THE SAME TO
BRIDGE CREEK, THENCE TO JAMES VANDAVERS TO KINSEY WIATTS, THENCE
TO JAMES HOLEMANS, THENCE TO BENJAMIN HALLS, THENCE TO OWEN
RECTORS, THENCE TO THE PUBLIC ROAD WHERE ELIGA HALE FAMILY LIVED,
THENCE ALONG SAID ROAD TO THE BEGINNING

THOMAS GREEN APPOINTED OVERSEER OF ROAD, HAVE MORGAN GREEN,
WILLIAM YORK, ISHUM HALE AND JOHN HALL WORK UNDER HIM

JOHN THOMAS, CLERK, PRODUCED IN OPEN COURT A SETTLEMENT MADE WITH
ROBERT OWENS, GUARDIAN OF MINOR HEIRS OF THOMAS INGRAM,
DECEASED...

SETTLEMENT OF WILLIAM WALKER, TRUSTEE MADE WITH WILLIAM FOSTER
AND WILLIAM WORTHINGTON WAS READ IN OPEN COURT...INSPECTED,
ORDERED TO RECORD

P. 241   REPORT OF A. B. CARNES, ET AL, JURY OF VIEW: THE ROAD
SHALL BEGIN AT THE MOUTHOF JOHN HUTCHESONS LAND AND RUN WITH THE
FENCE NOW STANDING ON THE LINE BETWEEN SAID HUTCHESONS AND
AQUILLA JOHNSON TO THE RIVER, THENCE WITH THE RIVER TO THE OLD
FORD, THENCE ACROSS SAID RIVER, THENCE TO THE MOUTH OF THE LANE
BETWEEN THOMAS AND ANDERSONS THROUGH SAID LANE WITH THOMAS FENCE
TO THE CORNER AND THENCE A NORTH CORSE TO DORSEYS...ORDERED THAT
ABOVE ROAD BE ESTABLISHED

P. 242   MARTIN A. SMITH PRODUCED A REPORT OF THE ASSETS AND
EFFECTS IN HIS HANDS AS GUARDIAN OF THE MINOR HEIRS OF JOSIAH
CRAWFORD, DECEASED...INSPECTED, ORDERED TO RECORD

REPORT OF JOHN THURMAN, ET AL, JURY OF VIEW: VIEWED AND MARKED
OUT ROAD COMMENCING AT OR NEAR B. F. BRIDGMANS, THENCE RUNNING BY
QUALS MILL, THENCE UP THE MOUNTAIN TO A CABIN BUILT BY DANIEL
QUALLS ON THE TURNPIKE ROAD, THENCE IN A DIRECTION TO HENRY
MILLERS PLACE NEAR THE COUNTY LINE BETWEEN BLEDSOE AND
RHEA...THINK ROAD OUGHT TO BE ESTABLISHED AND KEPT OPEN...SO
ORDERED BY THE COURT

P. 243   JOHN THOMAS, CLERK, PRODUCED IN OPEN COURT SETTLEMENT
MADE WITH ISAAC ROBERSON, GUARDIAN OF MINOR HEIRS OF WILLIAM LEE,
DESD...INSPECTED, ORDERED TO RECORD

ORDERED THATTHE COUNTY TRUSTEE REFUND TO STEPHEN HICKS, CLERK OF
BLEDSOE COUNTY CIRCUIT COURT, 9.81 1/4 WRONGFULLY PAID INTO THE
COUNTY TREASURY IN THE CASE   THE STATE VS FRANKLIN REAVELY

JOHN THOMAS, CLERK, PRODUCED IN OPEN COURT A SETTLEMENT MADE WITH
ISAAC ROBERSON, GUARDIAN OF MINOR HEIRS OF WILLIAM GREEN,
DESD...INSPECTED, ORDERED TO RECORD

WILLIAM BROWN AND ISAAC ROBERSON APPOINTED COMMISSIONERS TO
SETTLE WITH THE CLERK AND THE TRUSTEE FOR THE YEAR 1844

THIS DAY WYNN HOWL WAS BY THE COURT APPOINTED GIARDIAN OF THE
MINOR HEIRS OF DAVID SMITH, DECEASED. (ABSTRACTOR'S NOTE: THE
CLERK MAY HAVE OMITTED AN ORDER HERE, AS THE FOLLOWING IS IN THE
SAME PARAGRAPH.) WHEREUPON THE SAID BYRAM HEARD APPROVED IN OPEN
COURT WAS QUALIFIED AND ENTERED INTO AND ACKNOWLEDGED THE
FOLLOWING BOND...$1,000.00...SECURITIES, ISAAC ROBERSON AND
WILLIAM FOSTER

P. 245   FOLLOWING TAX LEVIED AND ASSESSED FOR YEAR 1844: FOR
COUNTY PURPOSES 5 CENTS ON EACH $100 WORTH OF PROPERTY
ON EACH POLL 25 CENTS
ON EACH MERCHANT FOR EVERY $1000 WORTH OF CAPITAL $1
ON EACH SHOW $30
ON EACH TAVERN $1
FOR POOR HOUSE 2 CENTS ON EACH $100 WORTH OF PROPERTY
ON EACH POLL 42 1/2 CENTS
ON MERCHANTS CAPITAL EACH $1000 $2.50
ON EACH SHOW $30
ON EACH STALION OR JACK THE SEASON 1 MARE

FOR JAIL   ON EACH POLL 5 CENTS
ON EACH $100 WORTH OF PROPERTY   1 1/2 CENTS
ON EACH MERCHANTS CAPITAL 75 CENTS ON EACH $1000

ALLOWANCE TO JOHN THOMAS, CLERK, SUM OF $60.24 1/2 CENTS FOR FEES

P. 246   THOMAS MANGU, ADMINISTRATOR OF ESTATE OF ROBERT FARR,
DESD, RETURNED INTO COURT INVENTORY AND AMOUNT OF SALES OF SAID
ESTATE...INSPECTED, ORDERED TO RECORD

COURT APPOINTED BYRAM HERD GUARDIAN OF AN EDICT HEIR OF DAVID
SMITH, DESD...SAID HERD APPEARED, ENTERED INTO BOND,
$200.00...SECURITIES, SAMUEL H. HUNTER AND SAMUEL RANKIN

ORDERED THAT WILLIAM FOSTER AND SAMUEL RANKIN, COMMISSIONERS, BE
ALLOWED $2.50 FOR SETTLING WITH STEPHEN HICKS, CLERK OF CIRCUIT
COURT FOR 1843

ALLOWANCE MADE TO BIRD THOMAS, SHERIFF...$47.60...FOR THE
DELINQUENT FOR THE YEAR 1843

P. 248   ORDERED THAT THE COUNTY TRUSTEE PAY TO GEORGE OXSHER
SEVENTY-FIVE CENTS THAT WAS OVER CHARGED IN THE COUNTY PART OF
HIS TAXES FOR YEAR 1843

P. 249   JOHN BRIDGMAN, WILLIAM WORTHINGTON AND SAMUEL MCREYNOLDS
APPOINTED COMMISSIONERS TO SUPERINTEND THE REPAIRING OF THE COURT
HOUSE, SUCH AS WINDOWS & DOORS...LET OUT SAME TO LOWEST BIDDER

JOHN THOMAS APPOINTED TO TAKE CARE AND KEEP SHUT THE DOORS OF THE
COURT HOUSE 1844 AND KEEP OUT ALL FURNITURE OR OTHER
OBSTRUCTIONS THAT DOES NOT BELONG TO SAID HOUSE

P. 250   PIKEVILLE   FEBRUARY SESSION   1844

PRESENT ON THE BENCH: THE WORSHIPFUL ESQ. JONATHAN WHITESIDE,
JAMES ORME, SAMUEL RANKIN

JOSEPH F. REED APPOINTED OVERSEER OF ROAD IN ROOM AND STEAD OF
GEORGE FINLEY

WILLIAM STEPHENS, WILLIAM THOMAS AND A. B. CARNES APPOINTED
COMMISSIONERS TO LAY OFF AND SET APART ONE YEARS PROVISION FOR
THE WIDOW OF ROBERT FARA, DESD...REPORT NEXT TERM

WILLIAM STEPHENS AND ELIGA M. HALE, ELECTED JUSTICES OF THE PEACE
FOR BLEDSOE COUNTY, APPEARED IN OPEN COURT...TOOK OATHS

JAMES ORME---WHO WERE APPOINTED AT LAST TERM, COMMISSIONERS OF
POOR HOUSE, APPEARED, WERE QUALIFIED

ORDERED THAT JOHN LOWERY, ANDREW WOODS, GEORGE MUNCY & SAMUEL
FRAILEY WORK UNDER ARON SWAFFORD AS OVERSEER OF PUBLIC ROAD

JESSE SHIRLEY APPOINTED TO SUPERINTEND POOR HOUSE FOR YEAR
1844...BOND, $1,000.00...SECURITY: BIRD THOMAS

ORDERED THAT WILLIAM RECTOR, OVERSEER OF PUBLIC ROAD, HAVE THE
FOLLOWING HANDS THAT BELONG TO JAMES WALKER, OVERSEER: MOSES
ORME, JAMES RECTOR, JOHN D. CLARK, ROBERT SHEILDS, GEORGE PRESLEY
& LANKIN PRESLEY

P. 253 A. H. COULTER, COMMISSIONER OF BLEDSOE COUNTY, TENDERED
HIS RESIGNATION AS CORONER...EXECUTED BY COURT

BYRAM HERD, GUARDIAN OF MINOR HEIRS OF DAVID SMITH, DESD,
RETURNED INTO COURT REPORT OF EFFECTS OF SAID ESTATE...INSPECTED,
ORDERED TO RECORD

ORDERED THAT IN ADDITION TO ORDER MADE AT LAST TERM APPOINTING
...COMMISSIONERS TO LET OUT THE REPAIRING OF COURT HOUSE HAVE
PANES TO WINDOW SHUTTERS TO THE LOWER WINDOWS ALSO TO SEAL UP THE
ENTRY NORTH EAST OF THE PASAGE AND A DOOR LOCK & KEY PUT IN PLACE
OF THE SAME

COURT ELECTED A CORONER IN PLACE OF A. H. COULTER...GEORGE
OXSHER...BOND, $2,000.00...SECURITIES: JOHN D. MORRIS AND JAMES
L. SCHOOLFIELD

GEORGE ALLEN APPOINTED OVERSEER OF ROAD IN ROOM AND STEAD OF
JACOB HORN

P. 255   FEBRUARY SESSION 1844

PRESENT ON THE BENCH: THE WORSHIPFUL JONATHAN WHITESIDE, ELISHA KIRKLIN, JAMES ORME, ESQ.

ORDERED THAT WILLIAM KERLEY, ADMINISTRATOR OF ESTATE OF DANIEL KERLEY, DESD, BE ALLOWED ONE HUNDRED DOLLARS OUT OF THE ESTATE UPON THE TIME OF HIS APPOINTMENT TO THE FIRST MONDAY IN MARCH 1844 FOR ATTENDING TO SAID ESTATE

WILLIAM BLAYLOCK PRODUCED IN OPEN COURT ONE WOLF SCALP...WOLF OVER FOUR MONTHS OLD...CERTIFICATE ISSUED

REPORT OF COMMISSIONERS APPOINTED TO SET APART ONE YEARS PROVISION FOR THE WIDOW OF ROBERT FAN, DESD...INSPECTED, ORDERED TO RECORD

PATRICK D. LAMB, ELECTED CONSTABLE FOR BLEDSOE COUNTY...APPEARED, WAS QUALIFIED....BOND, $4,000.00...SECURITIES: ADAM LAMB AND SAMUEL H. HUNTER

ORDERED THAT THE SHERIFF BRING TO NEXT TERM OF COURT TWO CHILDREN OF JULIAN FOSTERS

P. 258   APRIL SESSION 1844

PRESENT ON THE BENCH: THE WORSHIPFUL JAMES ORME, FOSTER, ISAAC ROBERSON, MARTIN A. SMITH, E. M. HALE, PHILLIP S. HUTCHESON, WILLIAM BROWN, SAMUEL H. HUNTER, JOHN F. GREER, GEORGE DAWSON, JONATHAN WHITESIDE, WILLIAM PAINE, SAMUEL RANKIN, JOSEPH HIXSON, AND WILLIAM GIBSON, ESQS.

ASBERRY HENEGAR APPOINTED OVERSEER OF PUBLIC ROAD IN ROOM AND STEAD OF JAMES SKILLERN

ORDERED THAT BIRD THOMAS, SHERIFF, BRING TO NEXT TERM OF COURT DANIEL THURMAN, SON OF CHARLES THURMAN, TO BE DEALT WITH AS THE COURT MAY THINK PROPER

FOLLOWING PRODUCED CERTIFICATES OF ELECTION TO THE OFFICE OFCONSTABLE OF BLEDSOE COUNTY: JAMES RANKIN, JOHN O. THOMPSON, E. L. RUDD, DANIEL WHITE, E. H. BOYD, ISAAC POTER, CHARLES B. WILSON, JOHN HAIL...OATHS...BONDS...SECURITIES FOR JAMES RANKIN: SAMUEL RANKIN AND MARTIN A SMITH...FOR JOHN O. THOMPSON: JOHN F. GREER, GEORGE DAWSON, CHATTER T. POLLARD

BOND OF E. H. BOYD, $4,000.00...SECURITIES, SAMUEL MCREYNOLDS AND
WILLIAM WALKER...SECURITIES FOR JOHN HALE: PHILIP S. HUTCHESON
AND JOHN BILLINGSLEY...SECURITIES FOR CHARLES B. WILSON: JAMES
ORME, JAMES A. TULLOSS AND WILLIAM WALKER...SECURITIES FOR E. L.
RUDD: JAMES A. TULLOSS AND THOMAS MANGU...SECURITIES FOR ISAAC
POTTER: BYRAM HERD AND JAMES A. TULLOSS...SECURITIES FOR DANIEL
WHITE: JAMES A. TULLOSS AND THOMAS MAUZEE

ALLOWANCE OF $7.50 TO GEORGE OXSHEER FOR HOLDING ELECTION IN THE
SEVERAL DISTRICTS OF BLEDSOE COUNTY ON 2ND MARCH 1844

GEORGE OXSHEER ELECTED CORONER OF BLEDSOE COUNTY FOR NEXT ENSUING
TWO YEAR BY THE COURT...APPEARED IN COURT, TOOK DIFFERENT OATHS
PRESCRIBED BY LAW...BOND, $2500.00...SECURITIES: JOHN F. GREER,
WILLIAM BRIANT AND SAMUEL OXSHEER

SAMPSON D. BRIDGMAN, ELECTED REGISTER FOR BLEDSOE COUNTY ON 2ND
MARCH 1844, APPEARED, TOOK OATH, ENTERED BOND...SECURITIES: JOHN
BRIDGMAN AND WILLIAM WALKER   (BOND, $12,000.00)

ON APPLICATION OF S. D. BRIDGMAN, THOMAS R. ROGERS APPEARED IN
OPEN COURT AND WAS QUALIFIED TO PERFORM DUTIES OF DEPUTY REGISTER

WILLIAM WALKER, ELECTED TRUSTEE FOR BLEDSOE COUNTY, APPEARED IN
OPEN COURT, TOOK OATH, PRESENTED BOND...$5,000.00...SECURITIES:
SAMPSON D. BRIDGMAN AND SAMUEL MCREYNOLDS

ALLOWANCE MADE TO S. D. BRIDGMAN FOR SEVEN DOLLARS, FOR
FURNISHING RECORD BOOK IN REGISTERS OFFICE

CALVIN MCDONOUGH APPOINTED OVERSEER OF ROAD COMMENCING AT JESSE
WALKERS SPRING BRANCHAND THEN RUNNING UP BUCKNER HOWARDS SPRING
BRANCH, INCLUDING ALL THE HANDS ON WILLIAM WALKERS AND BUCKNER
HOWARDS LAND SOUTHEAST SIDE OF SEQUATCHY RIVER

SUM OF FIVE DOLLARS EACH ALLOWED REVINUE COMMISSIONERS FOR 1844:
J. B. MCCLENDEN, WILLIAM GIPSON, JAMES ORME, PHILIP S. HUTCHESON,
M. A. SMITH, JONATHAN WHITESIDE, WILLIAM FOSTER, ISAAC ROBERSON,
SAMUEL H. HUNTER, AND JOEL WHEELER

ORDERED THAT THE SHERIFF SUMMONS THE FOLLOWING GENTLEMEN TO
ATTEND AS JURORS AT THE JULY TERM OF CIRCUIT COURT FOR BLEDSOE
COUNTY: GEORGE DAWSON, ROBERT RENFRO, WILLIAM GIPSON, JOHN F.
GREER, JAMES ORME, CRAVEN SHERILL, WILLIAM PAINE, JOSPEH
MCDOWELL, WILLIAM S. BROWN, JOHN BILLINGSLEY, A. B. CARNES,

MARTIN A. SMITH, WILLIAM STEPHENS, WILLIAM S. DALTON, PLEASANT
VERNON, JONATHAN WHITESIDE, LEWIS KEEDY, JESSEE COLBERT, OWEN
BRIANT, BUCKNER HOWARD, GEORGE REEL,M JOSEPH HIXSON, SAMUEL H.
HUNTER, A. C. WHEELER, BYRAM HERD,...CONSTABLE E. H. BOYD, JAMES
RANKIN

BIRD THOMAS, ELECTED SHERIFF OF BLEDSOE COUNTY FOR NEXT TWO
ENSUING YEARS, APPEARED IN OPEN COURT, TOOK OATHS, ENTERED INTO
BOND...$12,000.00...SECURITIES: JOHN B. THOMAS, JAMES ORME,
GEORGE F. JONES, WILLIAM STEPHENS...BOND FOR
$4,000.00...SECURITIES: JOHN B. THOMAS, JAMES ORME, GEORGE F.
JONES, WILLIAM STEPHENS...BOND FOR $2,000.00...SAME SECURITIES

ON APPLICATION OF BIRD THOMAS, SHERIFF, JAMES HIXSON WAS
APPOINTED AND DULY QUALIFIED DEPUTY SHERIFF

BY ACT OF GENERAL ASSEMBLY OF STATE OF TENNESSEE...26 JANUARY
1836...SUM OF $2,000.00 WAS APPROPRIATED FOR THE IMPROVEMENT OF
THE SEQUATCHIE RIVER IN BLEDSOE COUNTY, AND ALSO BY AN ACT PASSED
ON 25 JANUARY 1844..... COURT MAY VEST THE SUM IN WORKS OF
INTERNAL IMPROVEMENTS, EITHER ON ROADS OR THE RIVER, FOR THE
SUPPORT OF COMMON SCHOOLSOR IN ANY OTHER WAY FOR THE USE AND
BENEFIT OF SAID COUNTY...COURT VOTED ON APPLYING SAID SUM TOWARD
PAYMENT OF AMOUNT DUE AND OWING FOR THE COUNTY OF BLEDSOE...TO
PAY SAID TWO THOUSAND TO THOMAS CRUTCHFIELD TOWARD AMOUNT OWING
SAID CRUTCHFIELD FOR THE COURT HOUSE OF BLEDSOE COUNTY

P. 279 ORDERED THAT ROAD LEADING FROM VALENTINE SPRINGS TO HUGH
PIKE BE ANNULLED AND THE OLD ROAD FROM SAID SPRINGS BETWEEN ISAAC
HUMBLES AND J. M. ROBERSON FARM BE RECEIVED AND ESTABLISHED AS A
FIRST CLASS ROAD...HUGH PIKE APPOINTED OVERSEER

ORDERED THAT ALLEN MERRIMAN HAVE ALL THE HANDS ON THE EAST SIDE
OF THE STAGE ROAD ON E. M. HALES PLANTATION

JOSEPH PATTON APPOINTED OVERSEER OF ROAD IN ROOM AND STEAD OF
JOHN HINCH

P. 280   MAY SESSION 1844

PRESENT ON BENCH: THE WORSHIPFUL JONATHAN WHITESIDE, SAMUEL
RANKIN, JAMES ORME, WILLIAM BRIANT, SAMUEL H. HUNTER

JOHN THOMAS, CLERK, PRODUCED IN OPEN COURT SETTLEMENT MADE BY HIM
WITH WILLIAM WALKER, COUNTY TRUSTEE, SHOWING DISBURSEMENTS OF
COMMON SCHOOL FUND...INSPECTED, DERED TO RECORD

JOHN THOMAS, READ IN OPEN COURT SETTLEMENT MADE WITH WILLIAM R.
THURMAN, EXECUTOR OF ELI THURMAN, DECEASED...ORDERED TO RECORD

COURT ELECTED A RANGER FOR BLEDSOE COUNTY FOR TWO
YEARS...BENJAMIN F. BRIDGMAN...APPEARED IN OPEN COURT, QUALIFIED,
ENTERED INTO BOND...$500.00...SECURITIES: A. H. COULTER, WILLIAM
WALKER

JOHN NEWBY, AN ORPHAN, AGE FOURTEEN YEARS, BOUND TO HEZEKIAH
KERTIS TO WORK AS AN APPRENTICE UNTIL HE ARRIVES TO THE AGE OF
TWENTY-ONE YEARS...AGREEMENT OF KERTIS...AGREES TO GIVE SAID
NEWBY A FIFTY DOLLAR HORSE, TWELVE MONTHS SCHOOLING AND AT THE
EXPIRATION OF HIS TIME A GOOD SUIT OF JENES CLOTHES, EXTRA OF HIS
COMMON CLOTHES...SECURITY JOHN HAIL

THIS DAY A. M. ANDERSON APPEARED IN OPEN COURT AND TOOK AN OATH
TO SUPPORT THE CONSTITUTION OF THE US AND THE STATE OF TENNESSEE
AND AN OATH AGAINST DUELLING AND AN OATH TO PERFORM DUTIES AS
CONSTABLE FOR BLEDSOE COUNTY...BOND, $4,000.00...SECURITIES:
JAMES LLOYD AND WILLIAM ANDERSON

P. 284 COURT PROCEEDED TO ELECT AN ENTRY TAKER FOR BLEDSOE
COUNTY, FOUR YEARS...WILLIAM L. DALTON RECEIVED MAJORITY OF
VOTES...APPEARED IN OPEN COURT, QUALIFIED, ENTERED INTO
BOND...$5,000.00...SECURITIES: S. TERRY, JAMES ORME

ROBERT DWIGGINS APPEARED IN OPEN COURT, TOOK OATH TO PERFORM
DUTIES AS DEPUTY SHERIFF

ON APPLICATION OF WILLIAM L. DALTON, THOMAS R. ROGERS APPEARED IN
OPEN COURT AND WAS QUALIFIED AS DEPUTY ENTRY TAKER

P. 286 JUNE SESION 1844

PRESENT ON THE BENCH: THE WORSHIPFUL JONATHAN WHITESIDE, SAMUEL
H. HUNTER, SAMUEL RANKIN, WILLIAM BROWN ESQ.

ELIOT H. BOYD APPOINTED COMMISSIONER OF EDLY HARRISON AND THOMAS
GARDNERS TURN PIKE ROAD LEADING FROM EAST VIEW TO EDLY HARRISONS

JOSEPH DAVIS PRODUCED IN OPEN COURT SEVEN WOLF SCALPS...KILLED IN
BLEDSOE COUNTY...UNDER FOUR MONTHS OLD...CERTIFICATES ISSUED

JONATHAN ACUFF APPOINTED OVERSEER OF ROAD IN ROOM AND STEAD OF
THOMAS GREEN

P. 287   JESSE CARMACK PRODUCED IN OPEN COURT SIX WOLF
SCALPS...WOLVES UNDER FOUR MONTHS OLD, KILLED IN BLEDSOE
COUNTY...CERTIFICATES ISSUED

ORDERED THAT LUCY DAVIS BE ALLOWED TWO HUNDRED DOLLARS IF SO MUCH
THERE BE LEFT IN THE HANDS OF JAMES WILSON, ADMINISTRATOR OF
WILLIAM H. DAVIS, DECEASED AFTER PAYING ALL DEBTS THERE IS
AGAINST SAID ESTATE, FOR MAINTAINING 8 CHILDREN FROM THE 18TH
JANY. 1842 TO 3RD DAY OF JUNE 1844

JAMES MOONYHAM PRODUCED IN OPEN COURT SEVEN WOLF SCALPS ...WOLVES
KILLED IN BLEDSOE COUNTY...UNDER FOUR MONTHS OLD...CERTIFICATES
ISSUED

P. 288   ORDERED THAT JAMES WALKER BE RELEASED FROM THE PENALTY
IN A BOND HE ENTERED INTO AT THE MAY SESSION OF COURT, 1841 IN
THE CASE WHEREIN RUFUS L. ONEIL WAS BOUND UNTO SAID JAMES WALKER

ON APPLICATION OF JOSEPH HIXSON, IT APPEARED MARGARET HUGHS LATE
OF BLEDSOE COUNTY HAS DEPARTED THISLIFE INTESTATE...NEXT OF KIN
DECLINE TO TAKE UPON THEMSELVES TO ADMINISTER HER ESTATE...COURT
APPOINTS JOSEPH HIXSON ADMINISTRATOR...ENTERED INTO BOND...(NO
AMOUNT GIVEN)...SECURITIES: WILLIAM FOSTER AND SAMUEL H. HUNTER

P. 290 REPORT OF COMMISSIONERS APPOINTED AT JANUARY TERM OF
REPAIRING THE COURT HOUSE...HAVE RECEIVED WORK DONE PER
CONTRACT...$79.00

P. 291   JULY SESSION 1844

PRESENT ON THE BENCH: THE WORSHIPFUL JONATHAN WHITESIDE, JAMES
ORME, WILLIAM BROWN, GEORGE DAWSON, SAMUEL H. HUNTER, BYRAM HERD,
M. A. SMITH, WILLIAM FOSTER, SAMUEL RANKIN, ESQ

JOHN THURMAN PRODUCED IN OPEN COURT THREE WOLF SCALPS...WOLVES
KILLED IN BLEDSOE COUNTY, UNDER FOUR MONTHS OLD...CERTIFICATES
ISSUED

ALLOWANCE OF SEVEN DOLLARS TO STEPHEN HICKS, CLERK OF THE CIRCUIT
COURT FOR BLEDSOE COUNTY, FOR FURNISHING RECORD BOOK

JONATHAN PIKE RELEASED FROM SEVENTY-FIVE CENTS OF HIS TAX FOR
YEAR 1844, OCCASIONED BY OVER CHARGES IN VALUATION PAPERS

ALLOWANCE OF SUM OF ONE DOLLAR TO JOHN B. MURPHY FOR REPAIRING
THE JAIL OF BLEDSOE COUNTY

S. D. BRIDGMAN APPOINTED OVERSEER OF ROAD IN ROOM AND STEAD OF A.
R. THURMAN, AND IN ADDITION TO HIS HANDS, HAVE THE FOLLOWING TO
WORK UNDER HIM: E. L. REED, A. P. GREEN, JOHN B. MURPHY, JAMES
T. NANNY AND THOMAS R. ROGERS

ORDERED THAT BENJAMIN BRIANT, OVERSEER, HAVE FOLLOWING TO WORK
UNDER HIM: JOHN NICHOLS, BUCKNER HOWARD, WILLIAM ROGERS

ALLEN GREER RELEASED FROM SEVENTY-FIVE CENTS OF HIS TAX FEE FOR
YEAR 1844 THAT OCCASIONED BY OVER VALUING HIS LAND...SAME FOR S.
D. BRIDGMAN

COURT VOTED TO MAKE ALLOWANCE OF EIGHT DOLLARS TO BURD YOUNG FOR
FUNERAL EXPENSES OF SARAH MCCLAIN THAT DIED AT HIS HOUSE, TO BE
PAID OUT OF TREASURY OF THE POOR HOUSE

ALLOWANCE TO JOHN THOMAS, CLERK OF BLEDSOE COUNTY, $12.75 FOR
FEES RENDERED SINCE 1ST JANY. 1844

P. 294 ALLOWANCE OF $79.00 TO S. D. BRIDGMAN FOR REPAIRING COURT
HOUSE OF BLEDSOE COUNTY

ALLOWANCE OF $2.00 TO A. P. GREEN FOR REPAIRING THE WINDOWS OF
THE COURT HOUSE

JAMES PARSON RELEASED FROM A POLL TAX FOR YEAR 1844 OVER AGE

P. 295 ORDERED THAT MARY CLARK BE RELEASED FROM SEVENTY-FIVE
CENTS OF HER TAX FOR YEAR 1843

JURY OF VIEW: ROBERT BURKE, ELIGA M. HALEY, WILLIAM RENFRO,
WILLIAM RECTOR, BAZZEL HEDGECOTH, JAMES D. HEDGCOTH, WILLIAM
HEDGCOTH...TO LAY OUT A ROAD OF THIRD CLASS IN DIST

1...BEGINNING ON GORDONS AND BROWNS TURNPIKE ROAD ABOUT ONE QUARTER OF A MILE EAST FROM GEORGE DAWSONS, THENCE THE NEAREST AND MOST PRACTIABLE ROUTE TO THE CRAB ORCHARD...REPORT NEXT TERM

ALLOWANCE OF $25.00 TO JOSEPH NEWMAN, TO BE PAID OUT OF THE TREASURY OF THE POOR HOUSE

P. 296   AUGUST SESSION   1844

PRESENT ON THE BENCH: JONATHAN WHITESIDE, JAMES ORME, SAMUEL RANKIN, WILLIAM REDWINE

NELSON CRAWFORD APPOINTED OVERSEER OF ROAD IN ROOM AND STEAD OF THOMAS PRATOR

WILLIAM HENDERSON APPOINTED OVERSEER OF ROAD LEADING FROM JOHN HUTCHESONS TO ORVILL PAINE IN RHEA COUNTY, THE BOUNDS OF THE ROAD TO COMMENCE AT THE ELBOW OF THE MOUNTAIN AND ABOVE JOHN HUTCHESON, RUN TO RHEA COUNTY LINE...TO HAVE FOLLOWING HANDS: JACOB MITTS, H. M. MCNEW, JOHN MITTS, JAMES M. HENDERSON, JOHN L. HENDERSON, JOHN GREER, NATHANIEL MARLOW, NATHANIEL COULSTON, WILLIAM POLLARD AND JOHN A. GENTRY

JAMES SWAFFORD APPOINTED OVERSEER IN STEAD OF ASA JOURDEN...HAVE FOLLOWING HANDS: WILLIAM VERNON, WILLIAM DANIEL, INEZ DANIEL, SAMUEL LOWERY, ALLEN GREEN, THOMAS MATTHESS, STERLING PHILIPS, CUBESON PHILIPS, JOHN PANTHER AND JAMES IVY

JAMES ROBERSON APPOINTED OVERSEER IN STEAD OF HUGH PIKE

ORDERED THAT FOLLOWING GENTLEMEN BE SUMMONED AS JURORS TO ATTEND THE NOVEMBER TERM OF THE CIRCUIT COURT FOR BLEDSOE COUNTY: JAMES M. REAVISS, JOHN STUBS, JAMES WALKER, WILLIAM LOWDEN, CHARLES K. SHERILL, BURELL LEE, ROBERT WORTHINGTON SEGNR, WILLIAM MCDOWEL, JAMES R. BROWN, F. A. JONSON, THOMAS GREEN, S. L. ANDERSON, DAVID D. CARDER, AUDLY SKILLERN, J. B. THOMAS, THOMAS FOSTER, J. A. THURMAN, WILLIAM FOSTER, ISAAC ROBERSON, JAMES WALKER, BRIANT MERIMAN, JOHN B. CROZIER, JOHN GRAHAM, J. R. WHEELER, JONATHAN POPE...A. M. ANDERSON AND DANIEL WHITE TO WAIT ON COURT AS CONSTABLES

JOSEPH HIXSON, ADMINISTRATOR OF ESTATE OF MARGARET HUGHS DESD RETURNED INVENTORY AND AMOUNT OF SALES OF SAID ESTATE...INSPECTED, ORDERED TO RECORD

WILLIAM WALKER, TRUSTEE, APPEARED IN OPEN COURT, ENTERED INTO
BOND FOR THE SAFEKEEPING OF THE COMMON SCHOOL FUND FOR BLEDSOE
COUNTY...$2,000.00...SECURITIES: SAMUEL RANKIN AND JOSEPH HIXSON

WILLIAM FOSTER APPOINTED TO SETTLE WITH J. R. WHEELER, ADMR OF
ESTATE OF ELISHA THOMAS, DESD, IN PLACE OF JAMES A. TULLOSS WHO
WAS APPOINTED AT JULY TERM, 1843

SAMUEL RANKIN AND WILLIAM FOSTER APPOINTED TO SETTLE WITH J. R.
WHEELER, ADMR OF ESTATE OF ELISHA THOMAS, DECD, RETURNED IN OPEN
COURT THEIR REPORT...EXAMINED BY COURT, ORDERED TO BE RECORDRD

P. 300   SEPTEMBER SESSION 1844

PRESENT OF THE BENCH: THE WORSHIPFUL SAM RANKIN, JAMES ORME,
JONATHAN WHITESIDE

THIS DAY THE LAST WILL AND TESTAMENT OF JOHN FORD SEGR. WAS
PROCEEDED BY OATHS OF JAMES WALKER AND CHATTER T. POLLARD, THE
TWO SUBSCRIBING WITNESSES

JOHN B. CROZIER APPOINTED OVERSEER OF ROAD IN ROOM AND STEAD OF
RIGHT JOHNSON

MICHAEL MILLER APPOINTED OVERSEER OF ROAD COMMENCING AT VALENTINE
SPRINGS BRIDGE AND RUNNING TO THE FOOT OF THE MOUNTAIN THAT
INTERSECTS THE TURNPIKE ROAD AT THE FOOT OF THE MOUNTAIN BETWEEN
J. M. ROBERSON AND SAID MICHAEL MILLER.   IRA O. HUMBLE TO HAVE
ALL THE HANDS FROM OUR SPRING, JAMES ROBERSONS, GEORGE OXSHEERS,
LAUSON BEACH AND O. C. BEACH TO WORK UNDER HIM

P. 301   C. C. STRANAHAN APPOINTED OVERSEER OF ROAD IN STEAD OF
BENJAMIN BRIANT...JACOB KEEDY IN ROOM OF WILLIAM KEEDY

JAMES SWAFFORD APPOINTED IN STEAD OF ASA JOURDAN AND HAVE ALL THE
HANDS IN THE FOLLOWING BOUNDS: BEGINNING AT SAMUEL LOWERYS,
THENCE BY ALLEN GREENS, THENCE BY THOMAS MATHISS, UP WALDENS
RIDGE, ALL THE HANDS LIVING ON THE SIDE OF SAID RIDGE TO JAMES
IVYS ON THE DIVIDING LINE BETWEEN JAMES AND AARON SWAFFORD TO
WORK UNDER HIM AS OVERSEER

KELLY BARKER PRODUCED ONE WOLF SCALP...WOLF OVER FOUR MONTHS
OLD...KILLED IN BLEDSOE COUNTY...CERTIFICATE ISSUED

P. 302 ORDERED THAT C. J. MCDONOUGH, OVERSEER, HAVE HENRY L.
EVANS AND MONROE EVANS WORK UNDER HIM

ON APPLICATION OF SARAH OXSHEER, SHE IS APPOINTED ADMINISTRATRIX
OF ESTATE OF SAMUEL OXSHEER DESD...APPEARED IN OPEN COURT, WAS
QUALIFIED...BOND, $600.00...SECURITIES: GEORGE OXSHEER AND
WILLIAM BRIANT

JOHN THOMAS, CLERK, PRODUCED IN OPEN COURT A SETTLEMENT MADE WITH
ANNA COOK, ADMINISTRATRIX OF ESTATE OF WILLIAM R. COOK,
DECEASED...INSPECTED, ORDERED TO RECORD

JOHN THOMAS, CLERK, PRODUCED IN OPEN COURT SETTLEMENT MADE WITH
MAY MASSE, GUARDIAN OF MINOR HEIRS OF RICHARD MASSEE,
DESD...INSPECTED, ORDERED TO RECORD

P. 304 OCTOBER SESSION 1844

PRESENT ON THE BENCH: THE WORSHIPFUL JAMES ORME, JONATHAN
WHITESIDE AND SAMUEL RANKIN

I. N. ANDERSON TENDERED HIS RESIGNATION AS CONSTABLE...ACCEPTED
BY COURT

ALFRED HIDER APPOINTED OVERSEER OF ROAD IN ROOM AND STEAD OF
THOMAS L. MOYRES

JONATHAN CLARK APPOINTED OVERSEER OF PUBLIC ROAD IN ROOM AND
STEAD OF JAMES R. BROWN

COURT APPOINTED FOLLOWING GENTLEMEN JUDGES OF THE ELECTION TO BE
HELD ON 5TH OF NOVEMBER NEXT, FOR THE PURPOSE OF ELECTING
PRESIDENT AND VICE PRESIDENT OF THE UNITED STATES: JOHN
NARAMORE, GEORGE DAWSON, JAMES M. REAVISS, JOHN F. GREER, WILLIAM
GIBSON, JOHN FORD, JOHN TOLLETT, WILLIAM NAIL, ISAAC STEPHENS,
ALFRED SWAFFORD JOSEPH MCDOWEL, THOMAS L. MOYERS, JOHN HALE, JOHN
H. ACUFF, ISAAC S. ANDERSON, BIRD HENSON, SAMUEL MCREYNOLDS,
JAMES SKILLERN, VALENTINE SPRING, JAMES LLOYD, THOMAS SUTHERLAND,
WILLIAM BRIANT, JOHN H. SPEARS, A. H. COULTER, ARON HUGHS, RIGHT
JOHNSON, ALEXANDER LAMB, JOHN MCWILLIAMS, JAMES NICHOLS, JACOB
TETERS

ON APPLICATION OF BIRD THOMAS, SHERIFF, A. M. ANDERSON APPEARED

IN OPEN COURT AND WAS QUALIFIED AS DEPUTY SHERIFF

S, C, NORWOOD APPOINTED OVERSEER OF ROAD IN STEAD OF JAMES A.
TULLOSS

CALVIN MILLER APPOINTED OVERSEER IN STEAD OF JOHN STUBS

SARAH OXSHEER, ADMX OF ESTATE OF SAMUEL OXSHEER, DESD, RETURNED
IN COURT INVENTORY AND AMOUNT OF SALES OF SAID ESTATE...EXAMINED,
ORDERED TO RECORD

ORDERED THAT JURY OF VIEW APPOINTED AT JULY TERM OF
COURT...ROBERT BURKE, ET AL...MAKE REPORT AT NEXT JANUARY TERM

OCTOBER TERM   1844

PRESENT ON THE BENCH: THE WORSHIPFUL JONATHAN WHITESIDE, M. A.
SMITH, WILLIAM BROWN, E. M. HALE ESQ.

WILLIAM MCDOWEL APPOINTED OVERSEER OF ROAD IN ROOM AND STEAD OF
PETER SWAFFORD

JAMES RANKIN TENDERED HIS RESIGNATION AS CONSTABLE IN THE 5TH
DIST. FOR BLEDSOE COUNTY...ACCEPTED

ROBERT ACUFF APPOINTED OVERSEER IN STEAD OF JOHN M. BILLINGSLEY

P. 307   COURT PROCEEDED TO ELECT ONE OF THE COURT KORUM WHEREUPON
WILLIAM BROWN WAS DULY ELECTED

DECEMBER SESSION   1844

PRESENT ON THE BENCH: JONATHAN WHITESIDE, WILLIAM BROWN, JAMES
ORME, M. A. SMITH, WILLIAM BRIANT, JOSEPH HIXSON ESQ. JUSTICES &
C.

ON APPLICATION OF WILLIAM KEARLY THE COURT PROCEEDED TO APPOINT
GEORGE OXSHER GUARDIAN OF MINOR HEIRS OF DANIEL KEARLY,
DESD...APPEARED...BOND, $1800.00...SECURITIES: JESSE COLVARD,
WILLIAM WALKER, JAMES ORME

P. 309   WILLIAM THOMAS APPOINTED OVERSEER OF PUBLIC ROAD IN
ROOM AND STEAD OF JONATHAN BILLINGSLEY...IN ADDITION TO
BILLINGSLEYS BOUNDS, HE IS TO HAVE ALL HANDS ON THE WEST SIDE OF
THE ROAD ON JOHN HUTCHESONS FARM

JESSE SEARBERRY APPOINTED OVERSEER IN STEAD OF SAMUEL WHITE

JOHN THOMAS, CLERK, PRODUCED SETTLEMENT MADE WITH WILLIAM
KERLY...INSPECTED, ORDERED TO RECORD

A. B. CARNES APPOINTED OVERSEER IN STEAD OF ISAAC B. HENSON

JOHN THOMAS, CLERK, PRODUCED SETTLEMENT MADE WITH JOSEPH HIXSON,
GUARDIAN OF THE MINOR HEIRS OF JOHN HIXSON, DESD...APPROVED,
ORDERED TO RECORD

FOLLOWING GENTLEMEN APPOINTED REVINEW COMMISSIONERS FOR YEAR
1845: GEORGE DAWSON, JOHN F. GREER, JAMES ORME WILLIAM BROWN,
SAMUEL RANKIN, WILLIAM STEPHENS, ELIGA HALE, WILLIAM BRIANT,
JOSEPH HIXSON, JOEL WHEELER

FOLLOWING GENTLEMEN APPOINTED JURORS FOR MARCH TERM OF CIRCUIT
COURT FOR 1845:JOHN STUBS, GEORGE DAWSON, CHATTEN T. POLLARD,
WEATHERSTON S. GREER, JAMES ORME, CHARLES K. SHERILL, WILLIAM
BROWN, JOEL SEAGRAVES, ROBERT WORTHINGTON JUNR, JACOB MITTS,
JAMES WORTHINGTON, WILLIAM THOMAS, WILLIAM STEPHENS, JONATHAN
WHITESIDE, PLEASANT VERNON, ELIGA M. HALE, JESSE COLVARD, WILLIAM
BRIANT, JACOB REED, A. H. COULTER, BURTON LACESETER, S. C.
STANDEFER, JOSPEH HIXSON ESQ, ANDREW J. WHEELER, T. A.
POPE...CONSTABLES, JOHN HALE AND E. H. BOYD

JAMES ORME APPOINTED ADMINISTRATOR OF ESTATE OF RIAL H. MILLARD
DESD....ORME APPEARED IN OPEN COURT, QUALIFIED...BOND,
$400.00...SECURITIES: WILLIAM BROWN AND MARTIN A. SMITH

BENJAMIN HAMILTON, JOHN TOLLETT AND ISAAC STEPHENS APPOINTED TO
LAY OFF AND SET APART ONE YEARS PROVISION FOR THE WIDOW OF RIAL
H. MILLARD, MAKE REPORT NEXT TERM

CLERK OF COURT PRODUCED REVINEW BOND OF BIRD THOMAS,
SHERIFF...EXAMINED AND APPROVED$2,000.00...SECURITIES: JOHN B.
THOMAS AND JOHN BRIDGMAN...BOND, $4,000.00, SAME SECURITIES

P. 316 SAMUEL WHITTENBURG APPEARD IN OPEN COURT, MADE
AFFIDAVIT...A CERTAIN DEED OF TWO TRACTS OF LAND THAT WAS MADE BY
ARON SCHOOLFIELD AND RICHARD T. SCHOOLFIELD IS LOST OR
MISPLACED...CANNOT FIND SAME...DEED WAS MADE TO SAID WHITTENBURG

THOMAS MANFEE, ADMINISTRATOR OF ESTATE OF ROBERT FANN, DESD
RETURNED INTO COURT ADDITIONAL INVENTORY OR AMOUNT OF SALES OF
SAID ESTATE...EXAMINED, ORDERED TO RECORD

JAMES T. NANNY, DULY ELECTED CONSTABLE TO FILL THE VACANCY
OCCASIONED BY THE REMOVAL OF E. L. REED...APPEARED IN COURT, WAS
QUALIFIED...BOND, $4,000.00..SECURITIES: JOHN B. MURPHY AND
JAMES A. TULLOSS

PAGE 318 JANUARY SESSION 1845 6 AJN 1845

PRESENT ON BENCH: THE WORSHIPFUL ESQ. JUSTICE WILLIAM (?BROWN),
SAMUEL RANKIN, JONATHAN WHITESIDE, ELISHA KIRKLIN, JAMES ORME,
SAMUEL H. HUNTER, JOHN F. GREER, PHILIP S. HUTCHESON

ORDERED THAT PHILIP S. HUTCHESON AND SAMUEL H. HUNTER SETTLE WITH
THE CLERK, TRUSTEE AND CO. FOR THE YEAR 1845

ALLOWANCE OF $5.50 MADE TO A. P. GREEN

P. 319 COURT PROCEEDED TO ELECT CHAIRMAN FOR 1845...JONATHAN
WHITESIDE

COURT ELECTED A COURT QUORUM FOR PRESENT YEAR: SAMUEL H. HUNTER,
WILLIAM BROWN & WILLIAM FOSTER

JOHN LEE JUNR, DULY ELECTED CONSTABLE IN THE 7TH DIST., APPEARED
IN OPEN COURT, QUALIFIED...BOND, $4,000.00...SECURITIES: JAMES
A. TULLOSS, A. H. MONTGOMERY

ALLOWANCE OF ONE DOLLAR PER DAY FOR YEAR 1844 TO JONATHAN
WHITESIDE, SAMUEL RANKIN, JAMES ORME AND WILLIAM BROWN, THE COURT
QUORUM

P. 321 ALLOWANCE TO ISAAC ROBERSON AND WILLIAM BROWN,
COMMISSIONERS OF REVINEW FOR 1844, THE SUM OF $2.50 EACH FOR
SETTLING WITH STEPHEN HICKS, CIRCUIT COURT CLERKK

JOHN THOMAS, CLERK, PRODUCED SETTLEMENT MADE WITH ISAAC ROBERSON, GUARDIAN OF MINOR HEIRS OF WILLIAM GREER, DESD...READ AND ORDERED TO RECORD

JOHN THOMAS PRODUCED IN OPEN COURT A REPORT OF SAMUEL W. ROBERSON, TREASURER OF ACADEMY FUND...INSPECTED, ORDERED TO RECORD

WILLIAM FOSTER AND ISAAC ROBERSON APPOINTED TO SETTLE WITH MARTIN A. SMITH, TREASURER OF THE POOR HOUSE ESTABLISHMENT...MAKE REPORT AT APRIL TERM

JOHN THOMAS PRODUCED SETTLEMENT MADE WITH ISAAC ROBERSON, GUARDIAN FOR THE MINOR HEIRS OF WILLIAM LEE, DESD...INSPECTED, ORDERED TO RECORD

P. 322 JOHN THOMAS, CLERK, PRODUCED SETTLEMENT MADE WITH BYRAM HERD, GUARDIAN OF MINOR HEIRS OF DAVID SMITH, DESD...READ IN OPEN COURT...ORDERED TO RECORD

WILLIAM WORTHINGTON CAME INTO OPEN COURT AND PROSECUTED HIS PETITION PRAYING FOR A CHANGE OF THE PUBLIC ROAD LEADING FROM PIKEVILLE TO TOLLE TTS MILL ON THE SOUTH SIDE OF SEQUATCHIE CREEK. COURT APPOINTED JURY OF VIEW TO MARK SAID CHANGE: JOHN F. GREER, JAMES ORME, CRAVEN SHERILL WILLIAM FARMER AND ELIJAH TUCKER...SAME HAD SATISFACTORY KNOWLEDGE, PREPARED REPORT THAT THE PUBLIC ROAD BE CHANGED SO AS TO LEAVE THE OLD ROAD AT THE NORTH EAST CORNER OF THOMAS HAILS FIELD, TO THE WEST, RUNNING THENCE UP THE FLAT TO JESSE BROWNS HOUSE, LEAVING SAME ON THE EAST, THENCE UP THE LAYS SPRING BRANCH LEAVING WILLIAM WORTHINGTON HOUSE ON THE EAST, AND INTERSECTING THE OLD ROAD IMMEDIATELY ABOVE SAID WORTHINGTONS HOUSE...REPORT BEING UNEXCEPTED TO, CONFIRMED BY COURT

WILLIAM STEPHENS, PHILIP S. HUTCHESON AND F.A. JOHNSON APPOINTED COMMISSIONERS OF THE POOR HOUSE ESTABLISHMENT FOR YEAR 1845...CAME INTO COURT, WERE QUALIFIED

P. 323 F. A. JOHNSON APPOINTED TREASURER OF THE POOR HOUSE...BOND, $1,000.00...SECURITY: JOHN BRIDGMAN

ALLOWANCE TO JAMES T. NANNY, THE SUM OF $1.00, FOR REPAIRING THE LOCK ON THE JAIL DOOR IN BLEDSOE COUNTY

ROBERT OWENS APPOINTED OVERSEER OF PUBLIC ROAD IN ROOM AND STEAD

OF S. W. ROBERSON

P. 325 ON APPLICATION OF JOHN THOMAS CLERK, ALLOWANCE MADE FOR
$32.50, FOR EXEFICO AND OTHER SERVICES

ALLOWANCE OF $5.00 TO WILLIAM BROWN FOR GOING AND FETCHING THE
TWO THOUSAND DOLLARS FROM SPARTA THAT WAS APPROPRIATED TO PAYING
FOR THE COURT HOUSE

JAMES ORME, ADMINISTRATOR OF ESTATE OF RIAL H. M. HEARD, (SHOULD
BE MILLARD) RETURNED INVENTORY OF SAID ESTATE...INSPECTED,
ORDERED TO REDORD

ORDERED THAT THE FOLLOWING TAX BE ASSESSED AND COLLECTED FOR YEAR
1845:
TAX TO BE APPLIED TO COUNTY PURPOSES: 36 1/4
ON EACH WHITE POLE
ON EACH $100 WORTH OF PROPERTY   5
ON EACH $100 WORTH OF MERCHANTS CAPITAL   1.00
ON EACH SHOW EXHIBITED   30.00
ON EACH TAVERN HOUSE   1.00

TAX TO BE APPLIED TO THE USE OF THE POOR HOUSE
ON EACH $100 WORTH OF PROPERTY   2.

TAX TO BE APPLIED TO THE PAYMENT OF DEBT DUE FOR THE BUILDING OF
THE COURT HOUSE
ON EACH $100 WORTH OF PROPERTY   5
ON EACH POLE   20
ON EACH $1000 WORTH OF MERCHANTS CAPITAL   2.50
ON EACH SHOW   20.00
ON EACH STALION OR JACK THE SEASON PRICE OF ONE MAN(?)

TAX TO BE APPLIED TO THE REPAIRING THE COURT HOUSE
ON EACH POLE   6 1/4
ON EACH $100 WORTH OF PROPERTY   1 1/2
ON EACH $1000 WORTH OF MERCHANTS CAPITAL   10.

P. 327 APPEARS TO SATISFACTION OF COURT, FROM AFFIDAVITS OF
JAMES HENSON, AUDLEY M. ANDERSON AND ROBERT DWIGGINS, THAT THE
FOLLOWING NAMED PERSONS AGAINST WHOM THE FOLLOWING TAX WAS
ASSESSED FOR THE YEAR 1844, AND WHOLLY INSOLVENT, HAVE NO
PROPERTY, EITHER REAL OR PERSONAL IN THE COUNTY OF BLEDSOE OUT OF
WHICH SAID TAX COULD BE COLLECTED...
EDMUND SHELTON   .85
JOHN LEWIS   .85
JACOB SWANER   .85
LEVI SMITH   .85
DAVID HORN   .85

```
DAVID CUZZART            .85
DAVIS SKILES             .85
BIRD STRICKLIN           .85
SHEDE MOONEYHAM          .85
WILLIAM HARDIN           .85
NATHANIEL MARLOW         .85
THOMAS SIMMONS           .85
SIMEON FREMAN            .85
BRITON NICHOLS           .85
JOHN CARTER              .85
SPENCER OGLE             .85
DAVID RAWLINGS           .85
WILLIAM BOWMAN           .85
WILLIAM MYERS            .85
WILLIAM STUBS            .85
WILLIAM SUTTON           .85
PETER D. WILCOX          .85
ROBERT ABEL              .85
WILLIAM ALSISON          .85
ROBERT BAYER             .85
WILLIAM HIDER            .85
CHARLES LOWERY           .85
THO PRATER               .85
JOHN SWAFFORD            .85
PLEASANT BREWER          .85
WILLIAM BLALOCK          .85
ABLE BURDITT             .85
WILSON FULKINS           .85
JOHN SWAFFORD            .85
JACOB SULLIVAN           .85
CHARLES THURMAN JR.      .85
```

MAKING IN ALL, SUM OF 30.60

IT IS ORDERED THAT THE SHERIFF OF BLEDSOE COUNTY BE DISCHARGED
FROM ALL FURTHER LIABILITY ON THIS TAX LIST FOR 1844...

P. 329 APPLICATION OF THOMAS F. BARNETTE, STEPHEN C. STONE, JOHN
CAMPBELL, GEORGE THOMAS, WILLIAM KNIGHT, JOHN VICONY, & JOHN
PARKS, PETITIONERS, FOR A JURY OF VIEW TO VIEW AND MARK OUT ROAD
COMMENCING BEYOND BEDFORD B. SMITHS AT THE FORKS OF THE ROAD TO
INTERSECT THE OLD ROAD AT OR NEAR THOMAS OLD PLACE.   COURT
APPOINTED JURY OF VIEW: HIRAM J. STONE, HUBBERD BLALOCK, WILLIAM
C. MOSS, BEDFORD H. SMITH, GEORGE A. MOYSES, CHRISTOPHER MOYRES &
THOMAS F. BARNETT...REPORT AT APRIL TERM

ORDERED BY THE COURT THAT THE SLEDGE HAMMER APPROPRIATED TO
ELLIOTT H. BOYD AND WILLIAM ROGERS, OVERSEER, BE APPOINTED TO THE
USE OF A. H. COULTER, C. J. MCDONOUGH, C. C. STRANAHAN & THOMAS
GRAHAM, OVERSEERS, AND THAT SAID STRANAHAN BE APPOINTED TO SEE TO
GETTING THE HAMMER AND TAKING CARE OF SAME

A. H. COULTER, OVERSEER, TO HAVE JOHN HUGHS AND ALL THE HANDS ON HIS PLACE TO WORK UNDER HIM

P. 330   FEBRUARY SESSION   1845

PRESENT ON THE BENCH: THE WORSHIPFUL WILLIAM FOSTER, SAMUEL H. HUNTER, ISAAC ROBERSON, JONATHAN WHITESIDE AND WILLIAM BROWN

JOHN THOMAS, CLERK, PRODUCED IN OPEN COURT SETTLEMENT MADE WITH MARTIN A. SMITH, GURADIAN OF THE MINOR HEIRS OF JONAH CRAWFORD, DESD...INSPECTED, ORDERED TO RECORD

ISAAC ROBERSON AND WILLIAM BROWN RETURNED INTO COURT A SETTLEMENT MADE WITH WILLIAM WALKER, COUNTY TRUSTEE FOR YEAR 1844...INSPECTED, ORDERED TO RECORD

P. 331 ORDERED THAT JOSEPH B. MCCLENDEN BE APPOINTED TO TAKE IN A LIST OF TAXABLE PROPERTY IN THE FIRST DISTRICT OF BLEDSOE COUNTY IN THE ROOM OF GEORGE DAWSON OUT OF THE COUNTY

THOMAS SWAFFORD RETURNED INTO COURT A REPORT AS EXECUTOR OF ARON SWAFFORD...SAME APPROVED, ORDERED TO RECORD

P. 332   MARCH SESSION   1845

PRESENT ON THE BENCH: THE WORSHIPFUL JONATHAN WHITESIDE, WILLIAM STEPHENS, SAML. H. HUNTER, WILLIAM BROWN, SAML. RANKIN, JAMES ORME, M. A. SMITH, JOHN F. GREER, JOSEPH HIXSON, ESQ.

JOHN RECTOR APPOINTED OVERSEER OF PUBLIC ROAD IN ROOM AND STEAD OF JOSEPH F. REED...JESSE C. BROWN, IN ROOM OF EDWIN BEATTY

ORDERED THAT SHERIFF BRING TO NEXT TERM OF COURT DANIEL THURMAN, THE CHILD OF CHARLES THURMAN TO BE DEALT WITH AS THE COURT MAY THINK PROPER

P. 333 JONA..THAN ACUFF APPOINTED OVERSEER IN STEAD OF THOS. GREEN...CLABORN DAVENPORT, IN STEAD OF JAMES WALKER...DAVID REID, IN STEAD OF S. D. HARRIS

JESSE B. SHERLY APPOINTED BY THE COMMISSIONERS OF THE POOR HOUSE SUPERINTENDENT OF SAID POOR HOUSE...PRODUCED BONDS AND

SECURITY...APPROVED BY COURT, TOOK OATH   (BOND NOT RECORDED)

JAS. ORME, ADMINISTRATOR OF RIAL H. MILLARD, RETURNED IN OPEN
COURT AN INVENTORY OF SAID ESTATE...INSPECTED, ORDERED TO RECORD

P. 334 S. C. NORWOOD APPOINTED OVERSEER OF ROAD IN STEAD OF
JAMES A. TULLOSS...ANDREW AKING, APPOINTED IN STEAD OF ANDREW
SMITH P.335   APRIL SESSION 1845

PRESENT ON THE BENCH: THE WORSHIPFUL WILLIAM FOSTER, JAMES ORME,
WILLIAM PAINE, ISAAC ROBERSON, SAMUEL H. HUNTER, ESQ. & C.

JURY OF VIEW: ELIJAH M. HALE, WILLIAM BRIANT, S. D. BRIDGMAN,
JAMES LLOYD, WILLIAM WALKER...TO MARK OUT AN ALTERATION IN THE
PUBLIC ROAD LEADING FROM WALDENS RIDGE TO THE BRIDGE NEAR THOMAS
FOSTERS AND WHICH A. M. ANDERSON IS OVERSEER...RETURN AT THIS
TERM OF COURT

WILLIAM HASKEW APPOINTED OVERSEER OF ROAD IN ROOM AND STEAD
OFALLEN MERRIMAN

JACOB NICHOLS APPOINTED OVERSEER OF ROAD IN ROOM AND STEAD OF
JOHN LEE

ORDERED THAT THE ROAD LEADING FROM ISAAC STEPHENS TO INTERSECT
CHARLES LOWERYS ROAD BE DIVIDED AT JAMES HOLEMANS, AND THAT JAMES
HOLEMAN BE APPOINTED OVERSEER OF THE NORTH END AND HAVE ALL HANDS
ON THE NORTH END... PLEASANT RIGHT APPOINTED OVERSEER OF ALL
HANDS ON EAST SIDE OF HOLEMANS

FRANCIS HUGHS APPOINTED OVERSEER OF ROAD FROM JESEE WALKERS
SPRING BRANCH TO THE BRANCH BETWEEN FRANCIS HUGHS AND JOSEPH
HIXSON AND HAVE ALL HANDS THAT LIVE ON EAST SIDE OF CREEK, DOWN
TO THE BRANCH BETWEEN FRANCIS HUGHS AND DANIEL BOWMANS WORK UNDER
HIM

ALLOWANCE OF $2.50 TO JOHN B. MURPHY FOR REPAIRING THE JAIL DOOR
FOR BLEDSOE COUNTY AND FOR WOOD FURNISHED AT THE MARCH TERM OF
CIRCUIT COURT

ALLOWANCE OF ELEVEN DOLLARS THIRTY-SEVEN AND A HALF CENTS TO JOHN
THOMAS CLERK FOR ISSUING ORDERS & C

JURY OF VIEW: JOHN BILLINGSLEY, WILLIAM MCDOWEL, WILLIAM FARMER, PETER J. SWAFFORD, AND EDWIN BEATTY, APPOINTED TO VIEW AND MARK OUT A ROAD LEADING ACROSS THE VALY BY REUBIN BROWNS TO BAITYS MILL...REPORT NEXT TERM

JAMES G. SPEARS APPOINTED OVERSEER OF ROAD IN STEAD OF THOMAS GRAHAM

JOHN THOMAS, CLERK PRODUCED IN OPEN COURT DIFFERENT SETTLEMENTS WITH GUARDIANS...ONE WITH JOHN HUTCHESON AS GUARDIAN OF CATHERINE PETERS, ONE WITH WILLIAM FOSTER, GUARDIAN OF DAVID PAINES HEIRS, AND ONE WITH ROBERT OWENS, GUARDIAN OF THOMAS INGRAMS HEIRS...ALL READ TO THE COURT, ORDERED TO RECORD

JURY OF VIEW: E. M. EVANS, DAVID GILBREATH, JOHN B. CROZIER, ARON HUGHS, FRANCIS HUGHS, A. H. COULTER, JONATHAN POPE, APPOINTED TO VIEW AND MARK OUT A ROAD OF THIRD CLASS, COMMENCING AT JONATHAN POPES AND RUNNING AND PASSING BY DAVID GILBREATHS AND ARON HUGHS SO AS TO INTERSECT THE VALEY ROAD AT FRANCIS HUGHS...MAKE REPORT NEXT TERM

P. 338 REPORT OF COMMISSIONERS ON ALTERING THAT PART OF ROAD LEADING FROM R. BROWNS TO BEATTY MILL WHICH JESSE C. BROWN IS OVERSEER...IN OUR OPINION SHOULD BE CHANGED ACCORDING AS THE SAID R. BROWN HAS LAID OUT...CONFIRMED BY COURT

ORDERED THAT THE FOLLOWING GENTLEMEN BE APPOINTED JURORS TO ATTEND THE JULY TERM OF CIRCUIT COURT FOR BLEDSOE COUNTY FOR YEAR 1845: JAMES M. REAVISS, WILLIAM HEDGECOTH, JOHN F. GREER, NATHANIEL BRISTOL, JOHN HINCH, WILLIAM PAINE, SIMEON SELBY, HIRIAM J. STONE, WILLIAM HALE, JOSEPH MCDOWEL, ANDREW BILLINGSLEY, SAMUEL RANKIN, A. B. CARNES, JAMES A. TULLOSS, JOHN THURMAN, PRESTON MCCLENAHAN, THOMAS FOSTER, HASKEW, G. H. BILLINGSLEY, OBADIAH RIGHT, EPHRAIM M. EVANS, FRANCIS HUGHS, JOHN MCWILLIAMS, JAMES NICHOLS, JACOB TETERS...CONSTABLE ISAAC POTTER, JOHN S. LEE

P. 339 ORDERED THAT PART OF THE STREET OF WHICH D. J. ROLLINGS WAS OVERSEER BE ATTACHED TO ROAD LEADING FROM PIKEVILLE TO THE FOOT OF THE MOUNTAIN TOWARDS SPARTA AND THAT S. C. NORWOOD OVERSEER OF THAT ROAD COMMENCED AT THE BRIDGE IN PIKEVILLE HAVE ALL THE HANDS TO WORK UNDER HIM THAT BELONGED TO THE ABOVE NAMES STREET BOUNDS

ORDERED THAT WETHERSTON S. GREER BE ALLOWED TO ERECT TWO GATES ON THE ROAD LEADING BY GREERS MILL

REPORT OF JURY OF VIEW...ELIJAH M. HALE, ET AL...ROAD ON WHICH .
M. ANDERSON IS OVERSEER...IN OUR OPINION THE ROAD SHOULD BE
CHANGED AS FOLLOWS...TO CROSSING THE BRANCH ABOVE WHERE THE ROAD
NOW CROSSES NEAR TO KEEDYS MILL AND RUNNING TO THE RITE OF THE
HOUSE WHERE ABSLUM JOYS MOVED FROM A FEW DAYS SINCE AND STRIKING
THE OLD ROAD SOME FIFTY YARDS THIS SIDE...REPORT FAVORABLE,
CONFIRMED BY COURT

P. 340   ORDERED THAT THAT PART OF ROAD ON WHICH JACOB KEEDY IS
OVERSEER BE DIVIDED AT ALFRED WHITES , JAMES LLOYD APPOINTED
OVERSEER OF THE SAME DOWN TO SAID WHITES AND HAVE HIS OWN HANDS
AND ROLLING HIS SON AND THAT JAMES ROBERSON BE APPOINTED OVERSEER
OF THE LAWN AND UP THE BRANCH ABOVE TO WILLIAM SMITHS AND HAVE
ALL HIS HANDS TO WORK UNDER HIM AND THAT JACOB KEEDY HAVE ALL THE
REST OF THE HANDS IN HIS OLD BOUNDS AND KEEP TO THE BRANCH ABOVE
WILLIAM SMITHS

ORDERED THAT SAMUEL WORTHINGTON BE ALLOWED TO ERECT A GATE ACROSS
A PUBLIC PASS WAY THROUGH HIS PLANTATION

BOND OF BIRD THOMAS...$4,000.00, AS COLLECTOR OF PUBLIC TAXES FOR
1845...SECURITIES, PETER HOODENPYL AND JAMES ORME

JURY OF VIEW: JONATHAN WHITESIDE, PLEASANT VERNON, JOHN THURMAN,
BIRD THOMAS, JAMES LLOYD, JOHN MASSEY, B. F. BRIDGMAN...TO VIEW
AND MARK OUT AN ALTERATION IN THE ROAD LEADING FROM JAMES LLOYDS
TO QUALLS MILL...REPORT JULY TERM

WILLIAM FOSTER APPOINTED CHAIRMAN PROTEM

JURY OF VIEW: JOSIAH RAINS, E. H. BOYD, WILLIAM BOYD, JAMES G.
SPEARS, HENRY THOMAS, WILLIAM HASKEW, WILLIAM L. BROWN...TO
VIEW AN ALTERATION IN THE STAGE ROAD COMMENCING NEAR ALBERT PHELPS
AND TURNING TO THE LEFT SO AS TO PASS WILLIAM BRIANTS BRIAR FIELD
SO AS TO INTERSECT THE OLD ROAD NEAR THE CORNER OF WILLIAM
BRIANTS WHEAT FIELD...REPORT JULY TERM

JAMES ORME TENDERED HIS RESIGNATION AS JUSTICE OF THE
PEACE...ACCEPTED BY COURT

ALLOWANCE OF $5.00 EACH TO REVINEW COMMISSIONER FOR YEAR 1845:
J. B. MCCLENDEN, JOHN F. GREER, JAMES ORME, WILLIAM BROWN, SAMUEL
RANKIN, WILLIAM STEPHENS, E. M. HALE, WILLIAM BRIANT, JOSEPH
HIXSON, BYRAM HERD

ALLOWANCE OF $19.50 TO PETER HOODENPYL FOR SURVEYING THE COUNTY
LINE

ALLOWANCE TO M.A. SMITH, TREASURER OF POOR HOUSE AND JAMES ORME
AND WILLIAM BROWN, COMMISSIONERS OF POOR HOUSE FOR YEAR 1844...
FIVE DOLLARS TO SMITH AND $2.50 EACH TO THE COMMISSIONERS

ORDERED THAT THE TREASURY OF THE POOR HOUSE PAY A CERTIFICATE TO
S. D. BRIDGMAN FOR $79.00 FOR REPAIRING COURT HOUSE

P. 344   MAY SESSION   1845

PRESENT ON THE EBNCH: THE WORSHIPFUL JONATHAN WHITESIDE, WILLIAM
FOSTER, SAMUEL H. HUNTER, WILLIAM BROWN

JOHN LOWERY APPOINTED OVERSEER OF ROAD IN ROOM AND STEAD OF ARON
SWAFFORD

BENJAMIN LOWDEN COMMISSIONED JUSTICE OF THE PEACE IN THE SECOND
DISTRICT IN BLEDSOE COUNTY...APPEAREDIN COURT, QUALIFIED AS SUCH

JOHN THOMAS, CLERK PRODUCED IN OPEN COURT A SETTLEMENT WITH
WILLIAM WALKER COUNTY TRUSTEE ON ACCOUNT OF THE COMMON SCHOOL
FUND...READ IN COURT, ORDERED TO RECORD

P. 345 JOHN THOMAS, CLERK, PRODUCED IN OPEN COURT A SETTLEMENT
WITH WETHERSTON S. GREER ADMINISTRATOR OF THE ESTATE OF JOHN
KIMMER, DESD...READ TO COURT, ORDERED TO RECORD

CLABERN DEVENPORT, ELECTED CONSTABLE IN THE 2 DISTRICT, APPEARED,
QUALIFIED, ENTERED INTO BOND, $4,000...SECURITIES JOHN F. GREER
AND JOHN D. MORRIS

P. 347   JUNE SESSION   1845

PRESENT ON THE BENCH: THE WORHSIPFUL SAMUEL H. HUNTER, JONATHAN
WHITESIDE, WILLIAM STEPHENS, PHILIP HUTCHESON, M. A. SMITH, ISAAC
ROBERSON, SAMUEL RANKIN,. ESQ WILLIAM BROWN ESQ.

MARY CLARK APPEARED IN OPEN COURT AND ENTERED INTO BOND AND
SECURITY APPROVED OF BY COURT AS GUARDEAN OF MINOR HEIRS OF JOHN
CLARK DESD.

THIS DAY THE COURT PROCEEDED TO ELECT ONE OF THEIR BODY AS A
COURT CORUM IN THE PLACE OF WILLIAM FOSTER RESIGNED...JONATHAN
WHITESIDE, DULY ELECTED

P. 348   WILLIAM HIXSON SENR. PRODUCED IN OPEN COURT ONE WOLF
SCALP...WOLF KILLED IN BLEDSOE COUNTY, WAS OVER FOUR MONTHS OLD..
CERTIFICATE ISSUED

P. 349   JULY SESSION   1845

PRESENT ON THE BENCH: JONATHAN WHITESIDE, ELISHA KIRKLIN,
WILLIAM STEPHENS, ELIJAH M. HALE, ISAAC ROBERSON, SAMUEL H.
HUNTER, MARTIN A. SMITH, SAMUEL RANKIN, WILLIAM PAINE, P. S.
HUTCHESON, WILLIAM BROWN

THOS. MAUZY TENDERED HIS RESIGNATION AS TRUSTEE TO THE LAFAYETTE
ACADEMY...RECEIVED BY COURT...THOS. N. FRAZIER APPOINTED IN PLACE
AND STEAD OF MAUZY

JOHN THOMAS, CLERK, TENDERED HIS RESIGNATION AS SUCH
CLERK...RECEIVED BY COURT

JOHN THOMAS PRODUCED IN COURT THREE WOLF SCALPS...KILLED IN
BLEDSOE COUNTY, UNDER FOUR MONTHS OLD...CERTIFICATES ISSUED

P. 350   ELISHA BOLING PRODUCED IN OPEN COURT ONE WOLF
SCALP...WOLF KILLED IN BLEDSOE COUNTY, OVER FOUR MONTHS
OLD...CERTIFICATE ISSUED

JURY OF VIEW: JOSEPH B. MCCLENDEN, JAS. ORME, GEORGE DAWSON,
BENJAMIN L D N, JAMES M. REVICE, AND JOHN F. GREER...TO VIEW AND
MARK OUT A SECOND CLASS ROAD COMMENCING AT JAMES WALKERS AND TO
INTERSECT GORDONS & BROWNS ROAD NEAR THE CORNER OF NATHANIEL
BRISTOLS FENCE...MAKE REPORT THIS TERM

P. 351   ORDERED THAT M. A. SMITH, FORMER TREASURER OF THE POOR
HOUSE, PAY OVER ALL OF THE MONEY THAT IS IN HIS HANDS BELONGING
TO THE POOR HOUSE TO FRANCIS A. JOHNSON, THE PRESENT TREASURER
AND ALL BOOKS, PAPERS & C BELONGING TO THE ESTABLISHMENT

ALLEN L. PITTS APPOINTED OVERSEER OF ROAD IN ROOM AND STEAD OF
CLABERN J. MCDONOUGH

ALLOWANCE OF $30.00 TO JOSEPH NEWMAN...MONEY TO BE PAID OVER TO
JOHN F. GREER, TO BE PAID OUT AS HE MAY THINK PROPER

RAWLING THURMAN APPOINTED OVERSEER OF ROAD IN STEAD OF TENNESON D.
BRIDGMAN

BENJAMIN MCCLENDEN, DULY ELECTED A CONSTABLE, GAVE BOND &
SECURITY AND TOOK OATH...BOND, $4,000..SECURITIES: JAMES M.
REAVIS, GEORGE DAWSON, WILLIAM BROWN, BENJAMIN LODEN

P. 353 ALLOWANCE OF SUM OF FORTH DOLLARS TO BIRD THOMAS FOR
SUMMONING TWO HUNDRED AND FORTY-EIGHT JURORS AND TTWENTY
CONSTABLES TO ATTEND BLEDSOE COUNTY CIRCUIT COURT AT THE SEVERAL
TERMS FROM NOVEMBER TERM 1841 TO NOVEMBER TERM 1844

P. 354 ALLOWANCE OF $3.75 TO JOHN THOMAS FOR FEES AS CLERK OF
BLEDSOE COUNTY COURT

ALLOWANCE OF $5.00 TO GEORGE OXIER, CORONER OF BLEDSOE COUNTY,
FOR HOLDING AN INQUEST OVER THE BODY OF WILLIAM IVY

THIS DAY THOS. MAUZY TENDERED HIS RESIGNATION AS TRUSTEE OF
LAFAYETTE ACADEMY...RECEIVED BY COURT...THOS. N. FRAZIER
APPOINTED IN STEAD

CLABOURN DEVENPORT TENDERED HIS RESIGNATION AS CONSTABLE IN THE
SECOND DISTRICT...RECEIVED BY COURT

(LAST TWO ITEMS PREVIOUSLY RECORDED)

P. 355 WM. R. THURMAN, COMMISSIONED AS JUSTICE OF THE PEACE FOR
BLEDSOE COUNTY, APPEARED IN OPEN COURT, WAS QUALIFIED

COURT PROCEEDED TO ELECT A CLERK IN THE ROOM AND STEAD OF JOHN
THOMAS RESIGNED...WILLIAM M. ORME, DULY ELECTED...TOOK OATHS,
ENTERED INTO BOND, $10,000.00...SECURITIES, JAMES ORME, M. A.
SMITH, JAS. A. TULLOSS...SECOND BOND, $5,000.00...SECURITIES,
SAME...THIRD BOND, $5,000.00...SECURITIES, SAME

THIS DAY JOHN THOMAS PRODUCED IN COURT TWO SETTLEMENTS MADE BY
HIM AS SUCH CLERK...ONE WITH THOMAS MAUZY, ADMINISTRATOR OF THE
ESTATE OF ROBERT FARMER AND THE OTHER WITH BIRD HENSON, GUARDIAN
OF MINOR HEIRS OF JONATHAN HENSON, DECEASED...READ, INSPECTED,

ORDERED TO BE PUT ON RECORD

REPORT OF WILLIAM HASKEW, ET AL, JURY OF VIEW: ALTERATION WOULD
BE BENEFIT TO THE COMMUNITY...ORDERED THAT ALTERATION BE MADE AND
IT BE ESTABLISHED AS A ROAD

ORDERED THAT GEORGE WALKER BE EXEMPT FROM PAYING A TAX ON 30
ACRES OF LAND IN THE 10TH DISTRICT...SUM OF 63 CENTS...SAID LAND
BEING LISTED IN MARION COUNTY FOR TAXATION

ALLEN GREEN RELEASED FROM PAYING FORTY TWO CENTS AS A TAX. IT
BEING MADE OUT THAT SUM TOO MUCH

JURY OF VIEW: JOHN TOLLETT, CHARLES K. SHERILL, JOHN HINCH,
HENRY SHERRILL, JOHN D. MORRIS, GREEN J. HOLDEN, AND THOMAS
NAIL...COMMENCING AT OR ANY ZONE TO INTERSECT THE OLD ROAD AT OR
NEAR HOLDENS MILL...REPORT NEXT TERM

JURY OF VIEW: ROBERT BURKE, WILLIAM KEETON, ELIJAH KEETON,
BAZZEL HEDGECOTH, WILLIAM HEDGECOTH, PLEASANT HEDGECOTH...TO MARK
OUR A ROAD OF THE THIRD CLASS COMMENCING ON GORDONS AND BROWNS
TURNPIKE ROAD ABOUT ONE QUARTER OF A MILE EAST OF GEORGE DAWSONS,
THENCE THE NEAREST AND MOST PRACTIABLE ROUT TO THE CRAB
ORCHARD...MAKE REPORT NEXT QUARTERLY COURT

REPORT OFJURY OF VIEW...E. M. EVANS, ET AL...ROAD OF THIRD
CLASS...ESTABLISH THE ROAD NOW OPEN AND USED AS THE GENERAL PASS
WAY LEAVING THE STAGE ROAD AT JONATHAN POPES, CROSSING THE CREEK
JUST BELOW EVINS MILL BY WAY OF DAVID GILBREATH ROUND THE RIDGE
BENJAMIN HUGHS, ACROSS SAID RIDGE THROUGH GRAHAMS LAND BY ARON
HUGHS AND INTERSECTING THE OTHER VALLY ROAD BELOW FRANCIS
HUGHS...ORDERED BY COURT THAT SAID ROAD BE AND IS HEREBY
ESTABLISHED

P. 361 JOEL SEAGRAVES APPOINTED TO ADMINISTER ALL..GOODS AND
CHATTLES OF WILLIAM EVITT, DECEASED...ENTERED INTO BOND

GOERGE OXSHEER APPOINTED OVERSEER OF ROAD COMMENCING AT CONLEYS
OLD STORE HOUSE UP TO JAMES A. THURMANS AND TO HAVE THE FOLLOWING
HANDS: ALL THE HANDS ON GEORGE OXSHEERS FARM AND ALL THE HANDS
ON THE HALES FARM AND ALL ON THE NEAREST SIDE OF THE RIVER ON
MAJ. JAMES ROBERSONS FARM

JURY OF VIEW: JOSEP. B. MCCLENDEN, JAMES ORME, JAMES M. REVICE,
GEORGE DAWSON, BENJAMIN LOWDEN, JOHN F. GREER...TO VIEW A ROAD

THE SECOND CLASS COMMENCING AT JAMES WALKERS AND TO INTERSECT
GORDONS & BROWNS ROAD NEAR NATHANIEL BRISTOLS
FENCE...RE*PO*RT...FAVORABLE...ORDERED BY COURT THE ROAD BE
ESTABLISHED...JAMES WALKER APPOINTED OVERSEER

P. 362 FOLLOWING NAMED GENTLEMEN APPOINTED JUDGES OF THE
ELECTION TO BE HELD ON 7TH DAY OF AUGUST NEXT, FOR THE PURPOSE OF
ELECTING A GOVERNOR, MEMBER OF CONGRESS AND MEMBERSOF THE STATE
LEGISLATURE:
1ST DIST.   WILLIAM RUSH, SAMUEL MILLER, BAZZEL HEDGECOTH
2ND DIST.   JAMES WALKER, NATHANIEL BRISTOL, JAMES GIPSON
3RD DIST.   ROBERT WORTHINGTON, WILLIAM KERLEY, THOMAS GANAWAY
4TH DIST.   J. J. POPE, WILLIAM MCDOWELL, EZEKIAH CURTIS
5TH DIST.   JOHN BILLINGSLEY, SAMULE RANKIN, JOHN H. ACUFF
6TH DIST.   JAS. A. TULLOSS, A. R. THURMAN, S. C. NORWOOD
7TH DIST.   JAS. LOYD, THOS. FOSTER, JACOB KEEDY
8TH DIST.   WILLIAM A. BROWN, A. H. COULTER, JOSIAH REINS
9TH DIST.   S. C. STANDEFER, ARON HUGHS, HARDY LASITER
10TH DIST. JONATHAN AUSTIN, J. R. WHEELER, ELONSO SMITH

ON THE APPLICATION OF WILLIAM M. ORME, AND WITH THE CONSENT OF
THE COURT, JAMES A. TULLOSS IS APPOINTED DEPUTY CLERK...CAME INTO
COURT AND TOOK OATHS

PLEASANT RIGHT APPOINTED OVERSEER OF ROAD LEADING FROM ISAAC
STEPHENS TO INTERSECT CHARLES LOWERYS ROAD TO THE HARTH ROCK ON
THE SIDE OF THE MOUNTAIN, IN THE ROOM AND STEAD OF JAMES WALKER

ORDERED THAT THE ROAD LEADING FROM ISAAC STEPHENS TO CHARLES
LOWERYS ROAD BE DIVIDED AT THE HARTH ROCK AND THAT JAMES HOLMAN
BE APPOINTED OVERSEER OF THE NORTH END

ORDERED THAT JOHN B. MURPHY BE APPOINTED TO TAKE CHARGE OF THE
COURT HOUSE FOR TWELVE MONTHS

ORDERED THAT ORDER MADE ON YESTERDAY APPOINTED GEORGE OXSHEER
OVERSEER, AND DIVIDING THE HANDS BE RECEIVED. AND THAT SAID ORDER
BE NOT ISSUED.

P. 365   AUGUST SESSION   1845

PRESENT ON THE BENCH: THE WORSHIPFUL JONATHAN WHITESIDE, SAMUEL
HUNTER, WM.R. THURMAN, WILLIAM BROWN, WM. FOSTER, SAML. RANKIN,
WM. HIXSON

ORDERED THAT WILLIAM RODGERS PAY OVER THREE DOLLARS TO CHARLES C.
STRANAHAN THAT IS IN HIS HANDS FOR MAKING SLEDGE HAMMER FOR
PUBLIC ROAD

PLEASANT HIXSON APPOINTED OVERSEER OF ROAD IN ROOM AND STEAD OF
GEORGE ALLEN

DAVID D. CARDER, DULY ELECTED CONSTABLE, GAVE BOND, TOOK
OATH...BOND, $4,000...SECURITIES: JOHN THURMAN, BIRD THOMAS

FOLLOWING NAMED GENTLEMEN APPOINTED JURORS TO ATTEND THE NEXT
TERM OF CIRCUIT COURT: GEORGE DAWSON, E. G. HALEY, DANIEL BROWN,
JAMES WALKER, J. D. MORRIS, WM. R. THURMAN, WM. LEE, WM. L.
JONES, PETER J. SWAFFORD, EDWIN BEATTY, M. A. SMITH, N. ACUFF,
ELIJAH TUCKER, S. C. NORWOOD, BIRD PANKEY, SAMUEL VERNON, JAMES
ROBERSON, WILLIAM FOSTER, OWEN BRIANT, JACOB SKILES, JAMES
CONDREY, HARDY LASETER, ELMER SMITH, JAMES THOMPSON, WM. L.
DALTON AND D. D. CARDER, JOHN HALE, CONSTABLES TO WAIT ON COURT

BIRD PANKEY APPOINTED OVERSEER IN STEAD OF RAWLINGS THURMAN

JAMES L. REAVIS PRODUCED IN OPEN COURT ONE WOLF SCALP...WOLF WAS
KILLED BY JOHN FORD IN THE COUNTY OF BLEDSOE, WAS UNDER FOUR
MONTHS OLD...CERTIFICATES ISSUED

P. 363 SEPTEMBER TERM 1845

PRESENT ON THE BENCH: THE WORSHIPFUL JONATHAN WHITESIDE, SAMUEL
H. HUNTER, WILLIAM BROWN

SAMUEL VERNON APPOINTED OVERSEER OF ROAD IN ROOM AND STEAD OF
ASBURY HENNIGER

THIS DAY THE CLERK PRODUCED IN OPEN COURT SETTLEMENT MADE BY HIM
WITH JAMES HIXSON, ADMINISTRATOR OF ESTATE OF WILLIAM DAVIS,
DECEASED...INSPECTED BY COURT, ORDERED TO BE SPREAD ON RECORD

CLERK PRODUCED SETTLEMENT MADE BY HIM WITH MAY MASSIE, GUARDIAN
OF THE MINOR HEIRS OF RICHARD MASSIE, DECEASED...INSPECTED,
ORDERED TO BE SPREAD ON RECORD

GEORGE A. MOYRES PRODUCED IN OPEN COURT ONE WOLF SCALP...WOLF
KILLED IN BLEDSOE COUNTY, OVER FOUR MONTHS OLD...CERT. ISSUED

ALLEN GREEN APPOINTED OVERSEER OF PUBLIC ROAD IN ROOM AND STEAD
OF JAMES SWAFFORD

S. C. NORWOOD APPOINTED OVERSEER OF PUBLIC ROAD WORK DOWN TO THE
FORD OF THE CREEK INSTEAD OF TO THE BRIDGE

T. A. POPE APPOINTED OVERSEER IN STEAD OF JACOB NEWMAN

P. 370   OCTOBER TERM   1845

PRESENT: WILLIAM R. THURMAN, ISAAC RANKIN, WM. STEPHENS, WILLIAM
FOSTER, JONATHAN WHITESIDE, BYRAM HERD, SAMUEL HUNTER, P. S.
HUTCHESON, JOEL WHEELER

ORDERED BY COURT THAT JOHN KELTNER TAKE CARE AND KEEP AN ORPHAN
CHILD DANIEL F. THURMAN WITHOUT A CHARGE ON THE COUNTY FOR THE
SAME AND TO DELIVER THE SAID CHILD WHEN CALLED ON BY THE COURT

JOHN SWAFFORD APPOINTED OVERSEER OF ROAD LEADING SAMUEL
WORTHINGTONS TO BEALLEN

ORDERED THAT C. C. STRANAHAN, OVERSEER HAVE THE FOLLOWING BOUNDS
OF HANDS INCLUDE NEWT WALKER PLANTATION, WM. S. BROWN, ON S. SIDE
OF THE RIVER ISAAC ANDERSONS INCLUDING THE LAND ON THE EAST SIDE
OF HOWARD SPRING BRANCH TO THE TOP OF THE MOUNTAIN AND C. C.
STRANAHAN PLACE

P. 371   ALLOWANCE OF $1.75 TO S. C. NORWOOD, JAILOR, FOR
FURNISHING JAIL WITH LOCKS

ALLOWANCE OF $6.00 TO B. F. BRIDGMAN FOR FURNISHING THE CLERK OF
CIRCUIT COURT WITH A RECORD BOOK

ALLOWANCE OF $3.00 FOR THE PURCHASE OF A SLEDGE HAMMER TO BE USED
ON THE PUBLIC ROADS WHERE HALE AND CRAWFORD ARE OVERSEERS

ALLOWANCE OF $10.00 FOR REPAIRING BRIDGE ACROSS SEQUATCHEE RIVER
AT JOHN THURMANS...JOHN THURMAN AND BENJAMIN F. BRIDGMAN
APPOINTED COMMISSIONERS TO SUPERINTEND IN REPAIRING OF SAID
BRIDGE

ALLOWANCE OF $10.00 TO REPAIR BRIDGE ACROSS SEQUATCHEE RIVER AT VALENTINE SPRING...THOMAS FOSTER AND VALENTINE SPRING APPOINTED COMMISSIONERS TO SUPERINTEND REPAIRING OF BRIDGE

FURTHER ALLOWANCE OF $30.00 TO BUILD A BRIDGE ACROSS SEQUATCHEE RIVER AT PIKEVILLE...WILLIAM STEPHENS, BIRD THOMAS AND JAMES A. TULLOSS   APPOINTED COMMISSIONERS TO CARRY THIS ORDER INTO EFFECT

P. 373   THE STATE   )
              VS   )
         B, SMITH   )   BASTARDY

ORDERED BY THE COURT THAT BEDFORD B. SMITH PAY TO CLARISSA HENRY THE SUM OF $20.00 FOR THE FIRST YEAR, $15.00 FOR THE SECOND YEAR, AND $10.00 FOR THE THIRD YEAR FOR THE SUPPORT OF HER CHILD, AND ALL COSTS IN THIS SUIT...SAID SMITH CAME INTO COURT WITH JAMES SWAFFORD, ENTERED INTO BOND FOR HIS FAITHFUL PERFORMANCE

THE STATE   )
   VS   )
DANIEL SULLIVAN)   PEACE WARRANT

PROSECUTOR IN THIS CASE HAS NOT APPEARED AND STATE REFUSES TO PROSECUTE...CONSIDERED BY THE COURT THAT DEFENDANT GO HENCE...APPEARS JOHN MANNON IS PROSECUTOR, CHARGE FRIVILOUS AND MALICIOUS...JOHN MANNON TAXED WITH COSTS

JURY OF VIEW: ISAAC STEPHENS, JOHN TOLLETT, JAMES L. SCHOOLFIELD, WILLIAM PAINE, THOMAS SLOAN, JOSEPH PATTON...TO VIEW AN ALTERATION IN THE PUBLIC ROAD COMMENCING AT STEPHENS BRANCH WHERE IT CROSSES THE OLD ROAD NEAR TOLLETTS MILL, TO INTERSECT THE OLD ROAD NEAR WHERE STEPHENS FIELD CROSSES THE SAME...MAKE REPORT JANUARY TERM

ORDERED THAT ELIJAH HALE, OVERSEER, HAVE THE FOLLOWING BOUND AND HAVE ALL THE HANDS IN SAID BOUND: COMMENCING AT THURMANS MEETING HOUSE, THENCE TO NASON SWAFFORDS JUNR. NOW LIVES, THENCE TO THE CREEK, UP THE SAID CREEK, OPPOSITE WHERE JESSE DAY NOW LIVES, THENCE TO SAID DAYS, THENCE TO OWEN RECTORS, THENCE TO T. HALES, THENCE TO THE MEETING HOUSE THE BEGINNING

P.375 JURY OF VIEW: THOMAS SWAFFORD JUNR., ROBERT LEA, BURREL LEA, PETER J. SWAFFORD, WILLIAM MCDOWELL, JOSPPEH MCDOWELL, JOHN HANKENS...TO VIEW AN ALTERATION IN THE PUBLIC ROAD LEAVING THE OLD ROAD THIS SIDE OF JONATHAN CLARKS ON TOP OF THE HILL, TURNING TO THE RIGHT AND INTERSECTING THE OLD ROAD THIS SIDE OF HOWARD SWAFFORDS...MAKE REPORT AT JANUARY SESSION OF COURT

JURY OF VIEW: JOHN HUGHS, JOSIAH REINS, E. H. BOYD, THOS.
GRIMES, JOSEPH HIXSON, JONSEY LASETER, BIRD LASETER...APPOINTED
TO VIEW AND MARK OUT A ROAD OF 3RD CLASS TO COMMENCE AT OR NEAR
A. H. COULTERS, THENCE ACROSS SEQUATCHEE RIVER AT WALKERS MILL
LEADING ON ACROSS THE RIDGE THE BEST AND MOST DIRECT ROUTE TO THE
STAGE AT OR NEAR SAMUEL HUNTERS...MAKE REPORT AT JANUARY TERM

WILLIAM BROWN APPOINTED OVERSEER OF ROAD IN STEAD OF JOHN LEA

P. 376 JOSEPH DORTON, DULY ELECTED A CONSTABLE...TOOK
OATHS...BOND, $2,000...SECURITIES: CHARLES K. SHERRILL AND JAMES
A. TULLOSS

JAMES BROWN APPOINTED OVERSEER OF ROAD IN STEAD OF J. R. WHEELER

JURY OF VIEW: B. LEA, R. LEA, G. J. JONES, B. HAMILTON, WILLIAM
R. THURMAN...TO VIEW AN ALTERATION IN THE PUBLIC ROAD COMMENCING
AT G. F. JONES LAND, TURNING TO THE LEFT TO THOMAS SWAFFORD SENR.
AND INTERSECT THE OLD ROAD...MAKE REPORT JANUARY TERM

ON APPLICATION OF NANCY FARRAR, SHE IS APPOINTED GUARDIAN TO
WILLIAM H. FARMER, MINOR HEIR OF ROBERT FARMER, DECEASED...BOND,
SECURITY...APPROVED BY COURT

P. 378 NO FURTHER BUSINESS TO TRANSACT, COURT ADJOURNED UNTILL
COURT IN COURSE

P. 379 NOVEMBER SESSION 1845

PRESENT ON THE BENCH: THE WORSHIPFUL JONATHAN WHITESIDE, SAMUEL
H. HUNTER, WILLIAM BROWN, WM. FOSTER, ESQ.

WILEY MERRIMAN AND ALLEN MERRIMAN APPOINTED ADMINISTRATORS OF ALL
PROPERTY OF MARKUS MERRIMAN, DECEASED...CAME INTO COURT,
QUALIFIED...ENTEREDINTO BOND (NOT RECORDED)

ORDERED THAT JONATHAN WHITESIDE, SAMUEL H. HUNTER AND GEORGE
OXSHEER LAY APART ONE YEARS PROVISION FOR ELIZABETH MERRIMAN,
WIDOW, AND FAMILY OF MARKUS MERRIMAN, DECEASED...MAKE REPORT AT
NEXT COURT

JAMES H. HICKS CAME INTO OPEN COURT AND WAS QUALIFIED AS DEPUTY
REGISTER OF BLEDSOE COUNTY

WILLIAM M. ORME PRODUCED IN OPEN COURT RECEIPT FROM THE COUNTY
TRUSTEE...$3.57, REVINEW COLLECTED BY ORME FROM THE 1 MONDAY OF
JULY 1845 TO 1 DAY OF SEPT 1845

ORDERED THAT JOSEPH PATTON OVERSEER WORK TO THE CREEK AT TOLLETTS
MILL AND WIDOW JONES

JEFFERSON BALLARD APPOINTED OVERSEER OF ROAD IN STEAD OF WILLIAM
MCDOWEL...JAMES F. THURMAN, IN STEAD OF JACOB NICHOL...JOHN N.
MEYERS, IN STEAD OF ALFRED HIDER...WM. B. SCHOOLFIELD, IN STEAD
OF JOHN RECTOR

WILL OF BENNETT RECTOR OF COUNTY OF BLEDSOE AND STATE OF
TENNESSEE:
1ST. I GIVE TO MY DAUGHTER ELIZABETH RECTOR ONE BED & FURNITURE
AND ONE COW
2ND. I GIVE TO MY DAUGHTER MARY H. RECTOR ONE BED & FURNITURE
AND ONE COW
3RD. I GIVE TO MY SON JOHN RECTOR ONE COLT
4TH. I GIVE TO MY SON MARK RECTOR ONE COLT
5TH. I GIVE TO MY BELOVED WIFE SARAH RECTOR ALL THE PROPERTY I
AM POSSESSED AT MY DECEASED .EXCEPT WHAT I HAVE ABOVE NAMED AS MY
HORSE, BEST CATTLE, HOGS, SHEEP,POULTRY, LOOM, AND ALL
APPERTANCES THEREUNTO BELONGING TO THE SAME HOUSE HOLD AND
KITCHEN FURNITURE, FARMING TOOLS, AND GEARS FOR HORSES DURING HER
NATURAL LIFE AND AT HER DEATH SHOULD SHE LEAVE ANY PROPERTY &
WITHIT (?) SOLD AND THE PROCEEDS THEREOF EQUALLY DIVIDED BETWEEN
MY SEVEN CHILDREN, THAT IS TO SAY JAMES RECTOR, OWEN RECTOR,
WILLIAM RECTOR, ELIZABETH RECTOR, MARY H. RECTOR, JOHN RECTOR,
MARK RECTOR, AND LASTLY I DO HEREBY CONSTITUTE AND APPOINT MY
TRUSTEE FRIEND JAMES RECTOR AND WILLIE RECTOR EXECUTORS....THIS
24DAY OF MAY 1841...S/ BENETT (X) RECTOR...WITNESSES: MARK
STEPHENS, ISAAC STEPHENS

P 283 DECEMBER TERM 1845

PRESENT ON THE BENCH: THE WORSHIPFUL JONATHAN WHITESIDE, SAMUEL
H. HUNTER, WILLIAM BRYANT

REPORT OF JONATHAN WHITESIDE, SAMUEL H. HUNTER, GEORGE
OXSHEER...APPOINTED TO LAY OFF ONE YEARS PROVISION FOR ELIZABETH
MEREMAN, WIDOW OF MARK MEREMAN, DECEASED...SO MUCH OF THE EFFECTS
, CROPS AND PROVISIONS ON HAND AS WILL BE SUFFICIENT IN OUR
OPINION TO SUPPORT HER AND HER FAMILY ON YEAR FROM THE DEATH OF
HER SAID HUSBAND. FOLLOWING:
25 HEAD OF HOGS FOR EATING AND MAKING HER MEAT

150 BUSHELS OF CORN TO FATTEN THE HOGS
400 BUSHELS OF CORN FOR THE USE OF THE FAMILY
THE AMOUNT OF COTTON, WOOL, AND FLAX ON HAND, ALSO
WHAT LEATHER IDS ON HAND
4 HEAD OF MILCH COWS WITH SUFFICIENT FODDER AND SHUCKS TO WINTER
THEM FOR GROCERIES AND SALT
THE SUM OF THIRTY DOLLARS
ALSO THE POULTRY ON HAND AND TALLOW
ALSO SIX BUSHELS OF WHEAT AND WHAT POTATOES, TURNIPS AND CABBAGE
ON HANDS
THIS 7TH NOVEMBER 1845
IT IS ORDERED THE ABOVE NAMED PROPERTY BE VESTED IN THE SAID
WIDOW ABSOLUTELY

WILEY AND ALLEN MEREMAN, ADMINISTRATORS OF MARKUS MEREMAN,
DECEASED, RETURNED IN OPEN COURT AN INVENTORY AND AMOUNT OF SALES
IN SAID ESTATE...INSPECTED, ORDERED TO BE SPREAD ON RECORD

FOLLOWING NAMED GENTLEMEN TO BE SUMMONED BY SHERIFF TO ATTEND AT
MARCH TERM OF CIRCUIT COURT TO SERVE AS JURORS: GEORGE DAWSON,
CHARLES LOWERY, CHALTON J. POLLARD, WORTHINGTON S. GREER, JAMES
ORME, OWEN RECTOR, PETER J. SWAFFORD, PHILIP S. HUTCHESON, MARTIN
A. SMITH, JET JOHNSON, JONATHAN WHITESIDE, JOHN BRIDGMAN,
PLEASANT VERNON, SAMUEL MCREYNOLDS, WILEY MEREMAN, WILLIAM
FOSTER, JAMES LLOYD, WILLIAM BRYANT, BENJAMIN BRYANT, WILLIAM L.
BROWN, SAMUEL H. HUNTER, JOHN HUGHS, JONSY LASITER, JOEL WHEELER,
SAMUEL W. ROBERSON, AND E. H. BOYD AND DANIEL WHITE BE SUMMONED
TO SERVE AS CONSTABLES TO WAIT ON COURT

JAMES AUSTIN AND ELIJAH AUSTIN APPOINTED ADMINISTRATORS OF THE
ESTATEOF JONATHAN AUSTIN, DECEASED...CAME INTO OPEN COURT,
QUALIFIED

FOLLOWING NAMED GENTLEMEN NAMDE TO TAKE IN A LIST OF THE TAXABLE
PROPERTY FOR THEIR SEVERAL DISTRICTS FOR YEAR 1846: GEORGE
DAWSON, JOHN F. GREER, W. R. THURMAN, P. S. HUTCHESON, MARTIN A.
SMITH, JONATHAN WHITESIDE, WILLIAM FOSTER, WILL BRYANT, SAMUEL
H. HUNTER, JOEL WHEELER

ISAAC ROBERSON TENDERED HIS RESIGNATION AS JUSTICE OF THE PEACE
FOR BLEDSOE...RECEIVED BY THE COURT

JONATHAN POPE, JACOB TETERS AND BYRAM HEARD APPOINTED
COMMISSIONERS TO LAY OFF ONE YEARS PROVISION FOR ABY AUSTIN,
WIDOW AND RELICT OF JONATHAN AUSTIN, DECEASED...MAKE REPORT NEXT
TERM

THE WORSHIPFUL WHITESIDE, WM. FOSTER, W. R. THURMAN, WILLIAM
BROWN, SAMUEL RANKIN, P. S. HUTCHESON, WM. STEPHENS, SAMUEL H.
HUNTER, E. M. HALE, M. A. SMITH, WILLIAM BRYANT, JOSEPH HIXSON
AND BENJ. LOWDEN ESQ.

ALLOWANCE OF $8.50 TO JOHN BILLINGSLEY FOR TAKING CARE OF THE
COUNTY COURT AND FURNISHING WOOD AND HAVING FIRES MADE

ALLOWANCE OF $31.50 TO JAS. A. TULLOSS, DEPT CLERK OF THIS COURT
FOR SERVICE AS CLERK FROM THE 1 MONDAY OF JULY 45 TO 1 MONDAY
JANY. 46

P. 388   ALLOWANCE OF ONE DOLLAR PER DAY TO JONATHAN WHITESIDE,
SAMUEL H. HUNTER, WILLIAM BROWN AND WILLIAM FOSTER COURT CORUM
FOR YEAR 1845

ALLOWANCE IN A BILL CERTIFIED FROM THE CIRCUIT COURT, THE STATE
VS NANCY MCCARROLL FOR SUM OF $21.62 1/2

ALLOWANCE OF $5.00 EACH TO WILLIAM STEPHENS, P. S. HUTCHESON AND
ALLOWANCE OF $10.00 TO F. A. JOHNSON FOR SERVING AS COMMISSIONERS
OF THE POOR HOUSE FOR 1845...JOHNSON AS TREASURER

P. 389   ALLOWANCE OF $20.34 TO S. C. NORWOOD, JAILOR, FOR KEEPING
SIMEON FREEMAN AND ELIZABETH BOLTON IN JAIL BY ORDER OF HIS HONOR
JUDGE CANNON

THIS DAY THE COMMISSIONER OF THE POOR HOUSE, ALSO THE
SUPERINTENDENT, MADE A REPORT...INSPECTED, ORDERED TO BE
RECORDEDCOMMISSIONERS TO SUPERINTEND THE POOR HOUSE FOR PRESENT
YEAR: F. A. JOHNSON, WILLIAM STEPHENS, P. S. HUTCHESON...F. A.
JOHNSON APPOINTED TREASURER

COURT PROCEEDED TO ELECT ONE OF THEIR BODY AS CHAIRMAN FOR
PRESENT YEAR: JONATHAN WHITESIDE

COURT ELECTED THREE OF THEIR OWN BODY TO ACT AS A CORUM FOR THE
PRESENT YEAR: JONATHAN WHITESIDE, WILLIAM STEPHENS, SAMUEL
RANKIN

ON APPLICATION OF GEORGE C. WHEELER, HE IS APPOINTED

ADMINISTRATOR OF ...E. T. WHEELER, DECEASED...ENTERED INTO BOND,
DULY QUALIFIED

JAMES AUSTIN AND ELIJAH AUSTIN ADMINISTRATORS OF JONATHAN
AUSTIN, DECEASED, RETURNED INTO OPEN COURT AN INVENTORY AND
AMOUNT OF SALES OF SAID ESTATE...INSPECTED, ORDERED TO BE SPREAD
ON RECORD

ON THIS DAY COURT PROCEEDED TO LAY AND LEVY A TAX FOR THE PRESENT
YEAR FOR COUNTY PURPOSES ON EACH POLE   .40
ON EACH $100 WORTH OF PROPERTY   8
ON EACH $1000 WORTH OF CAPITAL FOR MERCHANTS   1.00
ON EACH SHOW   30.00
ON EACH HAWKING PEDDLER   10.00
ON EACH TAVERN KEEPER   1.00
FOR COURT HOUSE
ON EACH $100 WORTH OF PROPERTY   .07 1/2
ON EACH $1000 CAPITAL FOR MERCHANTS   2.75
ON EACH SHOW   30.00
ON EACH STALION OR JACK SEASON PRICE OF ONE MARE ---
ON EACH POLE   .27 1/2

P. 391 CLATEN GREER APPOINTED OVERSEER OF ROAD IN ROOM AND STEAD
OF ROBERT ACUFF...SAMUEL GALT, IN STEAD OF N. CRAWFORD...JAS.
ABLE, IN STEAD OF MICHAEL MILLER...WILLIAM HALE, IN STEAD OF
WILLIAM WORTHINGTON

ON APPLICATION OF WILLIAM S. DALTON, THOS. W. HALE APPOINTED
DEPUTY ENTRY TAKER...CAME INTO COURT, WAS QUALIFIED

SAMUEL H. HUNTER AND P. S. HUTCHESON, COMMISSIONERS OF REVINEW,
RETURNED SETTLEMENT MADE WITH WILLIAM WALKER,
TRUSTEE...INSSPECTED, ORDERED TO BE SPREAD ON RECORD

P. 392 WILLIAM RIGSBY APPOINTED OVERSEER OF ROAD IN STEAD OF
JAS. A. THURMAN

SAMUEL RANKIN AND WILLIAM FOSTER APPOINTED COMMISSIONERS OF
REVINEW TO SETTLE WITH THE CLERKS & CO. FOR THE YEAR 1846

E. CARNAHAN APPOINTED OVERSEER IN STEAD OF JESSE SCARBORRY

JAS. A. TULLOSS, DEPUTY CLERK, RETURNED INTO COURT A SETTLEMENT
MADE BY HIM WITH WM. R. THURMAN AS EXECUTOR OF ESTATE OF ELI
THURMAN...INSPECTED, ORDERED TO BE PUT ON RECORD

AMOS SIMMONS APPOINTED OVERSEER OF ROAD IN ROOM AND STEAD OF
JONATHAN ACUFF

THIS DAY ON APPLICATION OF AUDLEY M. ANDERSON, DEPUTY SHERIFF,
RETURNED INTO COURT FOLLOWING NAMES PERSONS AS
INSOLVENTS,,,SHERIFF TO HAVE FOLLOWING ALLOWED HIM AS TAXES THAT
COULD NOT BE COLLECTED FOR YEAR 1845:

GEORGE CHRISTIAN	1	POLE	75
JAMES DAVIS	1	"	75
JOHN K. HALL	1	"	75
A. J. MCNABB	1	"	75
LAWRENCE AUSTIN	1	"	75
LUKE PANNELL	1	"	75
HUGH PIKE	1	"	75
JOHN SLONN	1	"	75
WILL BURCH	1	"	75
BARTHOLOMEW ROGERS	1	"	75
DAVID COZZATT	1	"	75
JOSHUA HELTON	1	"	75
HIRAM WELCH	1	"	75

          MAKING IN ALL   9.75
ORDERED THAT THE SHERIFF HAVE AN AUDIT ON HIS SETTLEMENT FOR THE
TAXES DUE FROM HIM FOR YEAR 1845

P. 394 ON APPLICATION OF JOHN BILLINGSLEY, ONE OF JOHN HALES
SECURITY AS CONSTABLE, CAME INTO OPEN COURT AND REQUESTED THAT
SAID HALE GIVE ANOTHER BOND FOR HIS FAITHFUL PERFORMANCE, AND
THAT HE BE RELEASED FROM ALL FURTHER LIABILITIES ON THE SAID
HALES BOND...HALE CAME INTO COURT AND ENTERED INTO A BOND WITH P.
S. HUTCHESON AND STEPHEN HICKS...BOND, $2,000

JAMES A. TULLOSS RETURNED A SETTLEMENT MADE WITH GEORGE OXSHEER,
GUARDIAN OF MINOR HEIRS OF DANIEL KERLY, DECEASED

ALLOWANCE MADE , SUM OF $19.19, FOR COSTS AND FEE TO THOS. N.
FRAZIER, ATTORNEY, FOR PROSECUTING A SUIT IN THE CIRCUIT COURT,
THE TREASURER OF THE POOR HOUSE AGAINST THE FORMER TREASURER

JONATHAN POPE AND JACOB TETERS, APPOINTED TO LAY OFF ONE YEARS
PROVISION FOR ABY AUSTIN, WIDOW AND RELICT OF JONATHAN AUSTIN
MAKE FOLLOWING REPORT: 4 HOGS __ BUSHELS OF CORN AND BALANCE OF
CORN IN THE CRIB, ONE COW AND CALF, ONE SACK OF SALT, 100 POUNDS
OF SEED COTTON, TWO DOLLARS IN HAND, 2 HEAD OF SHEEP, 1 AXE, 2
BEDS AND FURNITURE, ALL THE FOWLS EXCEPT THE GEESE, 1 POT RACK, 1
SHELF AND SUNDRY ARTICLES, 1 BIG POT, 1 FLAX WHEEL, 1 BIG WHEEL,
1 PAIR OF CARDS, 1 WEEDING HOE, 1 LARGE BIBLE, 1 STACK OF OATS, A
FEW SMALL BITS OF LEATHER, $18.00 TO BUY SUGAR, COFFEE, PEPER,
SPICE, GINGER, 1 TABLE, 6 CHAIRS, 2 SMALL TRUNKS, SOME SPUN
THREAD, ONE PAIR OF AND IRONS...ORDERED THAT SAID SUM BE VESTED

ABSOLUTELY IN SAID WIDOW AS HER OWN PROPERTY

JOHN M. MURPHY, PETER HOODENPYL AND JAMES A. TULLOSS APPOINTED A
COMMITTY TO EXAMINE THE GUARD HOUSE...MAKE REPORT NEXT TERM
WHETHER IT WOULD BE BEST TO REPAIR THE HOUSE OR TO TAKE AWAY AND
BUILD ANOTHER ONE

P. 398   FEBRUARY SESSION   1846

PRESENT ON THE BENCH: JONATHAN WHITESIDE, WILLIAM STEPHENS,
SAMUEL RANKIN

GEORGE OXSHEER TENDERED HIS RESIGNATION AS CORONER FOR BLEDSOE
COUNTY...RECEIVED

JOHN S. LEA APPOINTED OVERSEER OF ROAD IN ROOM AND STEAD OF A. M.
ANDERSON

WILLIAM ORME ENTERED INTO BOND AND SECURITY FOR FAITHFUL
PERFORMANCE OF AN ACT PASSED BY THE LEGISLATURE, REGULATING
TESSLING HOUSES (?) BOND, $5,000.00...SECURITIES: JAMES A.
TULLOSS, F. A. JOHNSON

JESSE B. SHERLEY APPOINTED SUPERINTENDENT OF POOR HOUSE...ENTERED
INTO BOND...QUALIFIED AS SUCH

WILLIAM M. ORME, CLERK OF THIS COURT, PRODUCED SETTLEMENT MADE
WITH BYRAM HEARD...READ TO COURT, ORDERED TO BE SPREAD ON RECORD

ORDERED THAT THE REPORT MADE TO THIS COURT ABOUT THE GUARD HOUSE
...LAY OVER UNTILL APRIL TERM

ORDERED THAT EACH AND EVERY PERSON THAT TAKES OUT LICENSE TO
RETAIL SPIRITS OF LIQUOR PAY A TAX TO THE COUNTY OF TEN DOLLARS

P. 400 JAMES W. ENGLISH PRODUCED IN OPEN COURT ONE WOLF
SCALP...WOLF KILLED BY ENGLISH IN BLEDSOE COUTNY, WAS OVER FOUR
MONTHS OLD...CERTIFICATE ISSUED

JONATHAN POPE, ROBERT OWENS, JOHN B. CROZIER APPOINTED TO SET
APART ONE YEARS PROVISION FOR WIDOW GILBRETH, WIDOW OF DAVID
GILBRETH, DECEASED

WILLIAM RENFRO APPOINTED OVERSEER OF PUBLIC ROAD IN ROOM AND STEAD OF CALVIN MILLER

BOND OF JOSEPH HIXSON, ADMINISTRATOR OF ESTATE OF DAVID GILBRETH, DECEASED...$600.00...SECURITIES S. H. HUNTER AND AARON HUGHS

COURT PROCEEDED TO ELECT CORONER...A. B. CARNES...BOND, $2,000.00...SECURITIES: SAMUEL RANKIN AND WILLIAM STEPHENS

BOND OF JESSE B. SHERLEY, SUPERINTENDENT OF POOR HOUSE...$500.00...SECURITIES: ARON SWAFFORD AND H. POLLARD

SAMUEL RANKIN APPOINTED REVINEW COMMISSIONER OF 5 DISTRICT OF BLEDSOE COUNTY, IN PLACE OF M. A. SMITH, FORMERLY APPOINTED

P. 405 MARCH TERM 1846

PRESENT ON THE BENCH: THE WORSHIPFUL JONATHAN WHITESIDE, SAMUEL RANKIN, WILLIAM STEPHENS, PHILIP S. HUTCHESON

COMMISSIONERS APPOINTED AT LAST TERM TO LAY OFF ONE YEARS PROVISION FOR ELIZABETH GILBRETH, WIDOW AND RELICT OF DAVID GILBRETH DECEASED, PRESENTED REPORT...SET APART SO OF THE CROP AND PROVISIONS ON HAND AS WILL BE SUFFICIENT IN OUR OPINION TO SUPPORT HER AND HER FAMILY ONE YEAR FROM THE DATE (OF DEATH) OF HER HUSBAND...
THE BACON AND PORK SUPPOSED 400 LBS.
ONE COW AND CHOICE OF LOTS
2 SHEEP, CHOICE OF LOTS
ONE SOW, CHOICE OF LOTS
100 BUSHELS OF CORN, ONE AXE, ONE HOE, ONE BEE STAND, CHOICE OF THE LOTS. ALL THE FODDER ON HAND, SUPPOSED 200 BINDS. ALL THE CHICKENS AND GEESE, ONE SIDE LEATHER. FIFTEEN DOLLARS FOR COFFEE, SUGAR AND SALT. FURNITURE (CHOICEO. WHAT CHAIRS ON HAND, FAMILY BIBLE, ONE LOOKING GLASS, COOKING VESSELS, CUPBOARD, WARE & C. PAIL, ONE WASH POT, ONE POT RACK AND DOG IRONS. ONE SHOVEL, SPUN THREAD ON HAND, L SMALL WHEEL AND REAL...ABOVE SPECIFIED OREDERED VESTED IN THE SAID WIDOW ABSOLUTELY

ROBERT H. SNODGRASS PRODUCED OPEN COURT ONE WOLD SCALP...WOLF KILLED IN BLEDSOE COUNTY, OVER FOUR MONTHS OLD...CERTIFICATES ISSUED

P. 407 ON APPLICATION OF A. H. COULTER AND OTHER PETITIONERS TO HAVE A JURY OF VIEW, COURT APPOINTED FOLLOWING: A. H. COULTER,

S. W. ROBERSON, J. C. ROBERSON, JAMES LASITER, JOSEPH HIXSON,
DANIEL BOWMAN, JOHN MCWILLIAMS...TO VIEW AND MARK OUT A ROAD OF
THIRS CLASS COMMENCING AT S. W. ROBERSONS MILL AND RUNNING UP THE
VALLY TO INTERSECT THE VALLY ROAD AT OR NEAR DANIEL
BOWMANS...MAKE REPORT NEXT TERM

ORDERED THAT THOMAS SWAFFORD SENR. AND ELIZABETH SWAFFORD,
EXECUTORS OF WILL OF ARON SWAFFORD, BE AND ARE REQUIRED TO COME
FORWARD AT NEXT TERM OF COURT AND GIVE ADDITION BOND AND SECURITY

JURY OF VIEW: A. H. COULTER, JOSEPH HIXSON, SAMUEL W. ROBERSON,
J. C. ROBERSON, JAMES LASITER, DANIEL BOWMAN, SR., JOHN
MCWILLIAMS, HENRY HORN, JONATHAN POPE...APPOINTED TO VIEW AN
ALTERATION IN THE ROAD COMMENCING AT ROBERSONS LANE, THENCE TO
THE BACK LINE BETWEEN ROBERSON AND MACWILLIAMS LINE, THENCE THE
BEST WAY TO SEQUATCHEE RIVER TO THE OLD ROAD...MAKE REPORT NEXT
TERM

JURY OF VIEW: A. H. COULTER, S. W. ROBERSON, J. C. ROBERSON,
JAMES LASITER, JOSEPH HIXSON, DANIEL BOWMAN, HENRY HORN, JONATHAN
POPE...TO VIEW AN ALTERATION IN THE PUBLIC ROAD LEAVE THE OLD
ROAD AT THE CREEK BELOW THE OLD TOWN MILL AND TO INTERSECT THE
OLD ROAD NEAR THE GRAVEYARD...REPORT NEXT TERM

ORDERED THAT JAMES WALKER, OVERSEER OF THE PUBLIC ROAD FROM JAMES
WALKERS TO NATHANIEL BRISTOWS, HAVE THE FOLLOWING HANDS: WALTER
GREER, WILLIAM LOWDEN, AND HANDS (OF) PLEASANT LOWDEN AND WILLIAM
GREER

ON APPLICATION OF JOHN L. ROBERSON BY ATTORNEY...TO APPLY FOR
LICENSE TO PRACTICE LAW...COURT SATISFIED HE HAS OBTAINED AGE OF
TWENTY-ONE YEARS, HAS BEEN A CITIZEN OF BLEDSOE COUNTY FOR TWELVE
MONTHS, HAS ALWAYS DEMEANED HIMSELF AS A GOOD AND WORTHY CITIZEN
AND A MAN OF HONESTY AND MORALITY...ORDERED SAME BE CERTIFIED

JESSE CARMACK COMMISSIONED A JUSTICE OF THE PEACE FOR BLEDSOE
COUNTY...SWORN IN AS LAW DIRECTS AND TOOK HIS SEAT ON THE BENCH

LAST WILL AND TESTAMENT OF A. H. MONTGOMERY PRESENTED TO COURT BY
FOUR SUBSCRIBING WITNESSES, THOMAS MAUZY, THOS. W. HAIL, JOHN
BRIDGMAN AND STEPHEN HICKS...THOMAS N. FRAZIER AND JAMES A.
TULLOSS, EXECUTORS, GAVE BOND, $3,000.00...SECURITIES: WILLIAM
STEPHENS AND ISAAC ROBERSON

P. 411 O. P. SCHOOLFIELD APPOINTED GUARDIAN OF MINOR HERIS OF
DAVID SCHOOLFIELD...BOND, $100.00, SECURITY, ISAAC ROBERSON

IN BOND OF O. P. SCHOOLFIELD: CHILDREN OF DAVID SCHOOLFIELD:
JAS. L. SCHOOLFIELD AND PERRY A. SCHOOLFIELD

ORDERED THAT TREASURER OF POOR HOUSE PAY TO ISAAC HUMBLE THE SUM
OF $20.20

P. 412 JURY OF VIWE: ROBERT BURKE, E. M. HALEY, WILLIAM KEETON,
BAZZEL HEDGECOTH, WILLIAM HEDGECOTH, JAS. D. HEDGECOTH, JEFFERSON
KEETON...ROAD OF 1ST CLASS LEADING FROM GORDON & BROWNS ROAD NEAR
GEORGE DAWSONS LEADING THE NEAREST AND BEST WAY TO THE CRAB
ORCHARD...MAKE REPORT, APRIL TERM

P. 413   APRIL SESSION 1846

PRESENT ON THE BENCH: THE WORSHIPFUL JONATHAN WHITESIDE, WILLIAM
STEPHENS, WILLIAM FOSTER, SAMUEL RANKIN, PHILIP S. HUTCHESON,
WILLIAM BROWN, SAMUEL H. HUNTER, JOSEPH HIXSON, BYRAM HERD,
MARTIN A. SMITH, WILLIAM R. THURMAN, E. M. HALE, WILLIAM BRYANT
ESQ.

ORDERED THAT DANIEL KNON (?) BE APPOINTED OVERSEER OF ROAD IN
STEAD OF BENJAMIN HARRIS

FOLLOWING WERE ELECTED CONSTABLES FOR COUNTY OF BLEDSOE FOR THE
ENSUING TWO YEARS ON 7 MARCH 1846: JOSEPH DORTON, WILLIAM DAY,
BEDFORD B. SMITH, D. D. CARDER, JAMES S. PANKEY, JOHN LEA, ELLITT
BOYD, S. C. STANDEFER, GEORGE ALLEN

BONDS RECORDED...$4,000.00...SECURITIES FOR JOSEPH DORTON:CHATTEN
T. POLLARD, HENRY SHERILL AND JAMES A. TULLOSS.....SECURITIES FOR
WILLIAM DAY: M. A. SMITH, WILLIAM FARMER, JAS. A.
TULLOSS.....SECURITIES FOR BEDFORD B. SMITH: WILLIAM FARMER, P.
S. HUTCHESON, HUBBARD BLAYLOCK.....SECURITIES FOR D. D. CARDER:
PETER HOODENPYL, JAMES A. TULLOSS.....SECURITIES FOR JAMES G.
PANKEY: JAMES A. TULLOSS AND BIRD PANKEY.....SECURITIES FOR JOHN
S. LEA: BIRD PANKEY AND PETER HOODENPYL.....SECURITIES FOR CARL
C. STANDEPHER: WILLIAM WALKER, GEORGE OXSHER AND PETER
HOODENPYL.....SECURITIES FOR ELLIOTT H. BOYD: SAMUEL MCREYNOLDS
AND WILLIAM WALKER.....SECURITIES FOR GEORGE ALLEN: PLEASANT
HIXSON, PETER HOODENPYLE AND WILLIAM WALKER

AUDLEY M. ANDERSON, DULY ELECTED SHERIFF OF BLEDSOE COUNTY ON 7
MARCH 1846, FOR NEXT TWO YEARS...CAME INTO COURT ENTERED INTO
THREE BONDS, WHICH WERE INSPECTED, ORDERED TO BE SPREAD ON
RECORD...TOOK OATHS...BOND OF $4,000.00, SECURITIES WILLIAM
ANDERSON, JAMES LLOYD AND WILLIAM L. BROWN...SECOND BOND,

$2,000.00, THIRD BOND, $12,000.00, SECURITIES SAME AS ON FIRST

WILLIAM WALKER, ELECTED TRUSTEE FOR BLEDSOE COUNTY, ON 7 MARCH
1846 FOR ENSUING TWO YEARS, CAME INTO COURT, ENTERED INTO BOND,
TOOK OATH...BOND, $5,000.00...SECURITIES: WILLIAM L. BROWN AND
JAMES LLOYD

THOMAS W. HALE, ELECTED CLERK OF COUNTY COURT ON 7 MARCH 1846 FOR
NEXT FOUR YEARS, CAME INTO COURT, ENTERED INTO FOUR BONDS, TOOK
OATHS...1ST BOND, NO AMOUNT, SECURITIES: JAMES A. TULLOSS,
DANIEL F. COCKE, JOHN BRIDGMAN...2ND BOND, $5,000.00, 3RD BOND,
$5,000.00, 4TH BOND $10,000.00, SAME SECURITIES

P. 435 ORDERED THAT AMY LOWE, WIDOW AND RELICT OF ANDREW R. LOWE,
BE ALLOWED THE SUM OF SEVENTY DOLLARS FOR SUPPORT AND RAISING HER
TWO CHILDREN, TO BE PAID OUT OF A CLAIM SHE OWES THE ESTATE OF
SAID ANDREW R. LOWE, DECEASED

ALLOWANCE TO JAMES A. TULLOSS, DEPT. CLERK, SUM OF FOUR DOLLARS
AND 56 1/2 FOR SERVICE RENDERED

ALLOWANCE OF SIX DOLLARS TO STEPHEN HICKS FOR FURNISHING A RECORD
BOOK FOR THE CLERK OF CIRCUIT COURT

P. 436 ALLOWANCE OF FOUR DOLLARS TO JONATHAN WHITESIDE FOR
FURNISHING A RECORD BOOK FOR THE COUNTY CLERK

ALLOWANCE OF FIVE DOLLARS TO GEORGE DAWSON, JOHN F. GREER,
WILLIAM R. THURMAN, PHILIP S. HUTCHESON, SAMUEL RANKIN, WILLIAM
FOSTER, WILLIAM BRYANT, SAMUEL H. HUNTER, JOEL WHEELER, AND AN
ALLOWANCE OF SEVEN DOLLARS AND FIFTY CENTS TO JONATHAN WHITESIDE,
REVINEW COMMISSIONERS FOR YEAR 1846

ORDERED THAT ALL PERSONS THAT HAS BEEN DOUBLE TAXED IN THE 7TH
DISTRICT BE RELEASED FROM PAYING SAID DOUBLE TAX

P. 437 ALLOWANCE OF $2.50 TO WM. BROWN AND JAMES ORME, EACH FOR
THEIR SERVICES AS COMMISSIONERS OF THE POOR HOUSE FOR YEAR 1844
AND M. A. SMITH, $5.00, FOR SERVICE AS TREASURER OF POOR HOUSE
FOR YEAR 1844

APPEARING THAT LEVI GREEN IS NOT ABLE TO MAKE A LIVING BY MANUAL
LABOR...COURT ISSUED LICENSE TO HAWK AND PEDDLE MERCHANDISE, HE

FIRST HAVING COMPLIED WITH ACT OF GENERAL ASSEMBLY, PASSED ON 4
JANY. 1838

P. 438   DANIEL SUTHERLAND APPOINTED OVERSEER OF ROAD IN STEAD OF
WILLIAM HUMBLE...BENJAMIN HARRIS, IN STEAD OF DAVID READ...DANIEL
F. COCKE, IN STEAD OF S. C. NORWOOD

REPORT OF JURY OF VIEW...CONFIRMED...ORDERED THAT ROAD LEADING
FROM S. W. ROBERSONS MILL INTERSECT AT DANIEL BOWMANS

REPORT OF JURY OF VIEW...CONFIRMED...ORDERED THAT ALTERATION BE
ESTABLISHED...LEAVING THE OLD ROAD AT THE CREEK AND INTERSECTING
STAGE ROAD AT THE GRAVE YARD

JURY OF VIEW REPORT...FAVORABLE TO ALTERATION IN ROAD BETWEEN
ROBERT WORTHINGTON SR. AND THOMAS SWAFFORD, SR...ORDERED
ESTABLISHED

ORDERED THAT THE SHERIFF SUMMONS THE FOLLOWING NAMED GENTLEMEN TO
ATTEND AS JURORS AT JULY TERM OF CIRCUIT COURT: WM. RENFRO, W.
RUSH, NATHANIEL BRISTOW, BENJAMIN LODEN, C. K. SHERILL, JOHN
TOLLETT, BURRELL LEA, SAMUEL WORTHINGTON JUNR., THOMAS SWAFFORD
JUNR., COL. WM. BROWN, SAMUEL RANKIN, ARON SWAFFORD, J. M.
BILLINGSLEY, WILLIAM STEPHENS, JAMES A. TULLOSS, WILLIAM VERNON,
O. P. SCHOOLFIELD, E. M. HALE, JOSIAH GRAHAM, JONATHAN POPE,
JAMES THOMAS...AND THAT S. C. STANDEFER AND WILLIAM DAY BE
SUMMONED TO WAIT ON THE COURT

J. HENRY SHERILL, COMMISSIONED JUSTICE OF THE PEACE FOR BLEDSOE
COUNTY, CAME INTO COURT, TOOK OATHS, AND TOOK HIS SEAT ON THE
BENCH

P. 440   O. P. SCHOOLFIELD APPOINTED OVERSEER OF ROAD LEADING FROM
SPRINGS ROAD TO ENTER THE TURNPIKE ROAD ON THE SIDE OF THE
MOUNTAIN, TO BE A THIRD CLASS ROAD...ALL HANDS ON PLACE OWNED BY
SCHOOLFIELD WORK ON SAID ROAD

ORDERED THAT ROAD WHERE WILLIAM HASKEW IS OVERSEER BE DIVIDED BY
WILLIAM HASKEW AND GEORGE OXSHEER...ALSO THE HANDS, AND THAT
WILEY MEREMAN AND GEORGE OXSHEER BE APPOINTED OVERSEERS ON SAID
ROAD...MEREMAN, THE LOWER, AND OXSHEER THE UPPER...THE HANDS ON
JAMES ROBERSONS LAND ON THE NORTHWEST SIDE OF THE RIVER WORK THE
LOWER END, AND ALL THE HANDS ON GEORGE OXSHEERS LAND WORK ON
STAGE ROAD TO EXTEND THE LOWER END OF ROAD DOWN AS FAR AS PHELPS

ORDERED BY COURT THAT ALFRED HUTCHESON IS APPOINTED TO ASK AND
DEMAND OF WILLIAM HUTCHESON, ADMINISTRATOR, THE FULL SUM OF MONEY
THAT WAS LEFT WITH WILLIAM HUTCHESON IN HIS LIFETIME BY REBECCA
HUTCHESON...SAID ALFRED HUTCHESON IS OUTHORISED TO RECEIPT FOR
SAME AND TO KEEP SAID SUM TO THE ORDER OF SAID REBECCA HUTCHESON

JAMES A. TULLOSS PRODUCED IN OPEN COURT TWO SETTLEMENTS MADE WITH
ISAAC ROBERSON, GUARDIAN OF MINOR HEIRS OF WILLIAM GREER,
DECEASED AND WILLIAM LEA, DECEASED

THOMAS N. FRAZIER AND JAMES A. TULLOSS GIVEN UNTILL NEXT TERM OF
COURT TO RETURN INVENTORY OF ESTATE OF A. H. MONTGOMERY, DECEASED

COMMISSIONERS ISAAC STEPHENS, BENJAMIN HAMILTON, JAMES ORME, JOHN
TOLLETT APPOINTED TO LAY OFF ONE YEARS PROVISION FOR NANCY GUALT,
WIDOW AND RELICT OF RICHARD GAULT, DECEASED

JURY OF VIEW: ISAAC STEPHENS, JAMES L. SCHOOLFIELD, JOHN
TOLLETT, JOSEPH PATTON, THOMAS SLOAN, WILLIAM KERLEY...TO VIEW A
ROAD BEGINNING AT ISAAC STEPHENS BRANCH TO INTERSECT THE OLD ROAD
ON TOP OF THE HILL...MAKE REPORT NEXT TERM

P. 442 H. COX, OVERSEER OF ROAD LEADING FROM THE COVE TO THE TOP
OF THE MOUNTAIN TO HAVE FOLLOWING HANDS: DANIEL BROWN, JAMES
REAVICE, M. D. ELLISON, GEORGE COX, M. ROMINES, W. HAMILTON, JOHN
COX, J. DORTON, WILLIAM HOLLOWAY, WILLIAM LIVELY

JAMES A. TULLOSS PRODUCED IN OPEN COURT SETTLEMENT MADE WITH
ROBERT OWENS, GUARDIAN OF MINOR HEIRS OF THOS INGRAM,
DECEASED...INSPECTED, ORDERED TO BE PUT ON RECORD

CALENIS LAMB APPOINTED OVERSEER OF ROAD IN STEAD OF JAMES G.
SPEARS

WILLIAM HASKEW AND JAMES G. SPEARS RETURNED INTO COURT THE
FOLLOWING INSTRUMENT OF RITING:
TO THE COUNTY COURT-THIS IS TO CERTIFY THAT THE NEW ROAD MAID BY
WILLIAM BRYANT IS IN GOOD REPAIR AND WE OVERSEERS ACCEPT THE SAME
THIS 4 DAY OF MARCH 1846

P. 444 JAMES WALKER APPOINTED OVERSEER OF ROAD FROM JESSEE
WALKERS SPRING BRANCH BETWEEN JOSEPH HIXSONS AND FRANK HUGHS

WM. R. WRITT APPOINTED OVERSEER OF ROAD LEADING FROM ISAAC

STEPHENS TO INTERSECT WITH CHARLES LOWERYS

E. M. EVANS APPOINTED OVERSEER OF ROAD IN ROOM OF JOHN B. CROZIER

APPEARING TO COURT, ANDREW MCDONOUGH WAS PENSIONER OF THE US AT
THE RATE OF THIRTY SIX DOLLARS AND THIRTY SIX CENTS PER ANNUM,
THAT HE DIED IN MARION COUNTY TENNESSEE ON THE 20 OF JANY. 1846,
THAT HE LEFT NO WIDOW, AND THAT HE LEFT THREE CHILDREN WHOSE
NAMES ARE ELIZABETH LANGLEY, ANDREW MCDONOUGH AND CALVIN
MCDONOUGH, WHO RESIDE IN THIS STATE...ORDERED THAT THE CLERK
CERTIFY ABOVE FACTS AS REQUIRED BY THE REGULATIONS OF THE WAR
DEPARTMENT

GEORGE DAWSON ENTERED HIS RESIGNATION WHICH WAS RECORDED BY THE
COURT AS JUSTICE OF THE PEACE

P. 445   EPHRAIM WELCH APPOINTED OVERSEER OF ROAD IN STEAD OF
JAMES BROWN

ALFRED M. SKILLERN APPOINTED OVERSEER OF ROAD IN ROOM AND STEAD
OF JAMES ABLE-IN 7TH DISTRICT

BOND OF JOHN B. MURPHY, CORONER OF BLEDSOE
COUNTY...$2,000.00...SECURITIES: PETER HOODENPYL AND WILLIAM M.
ORME

BOND OF BENJAMIN F. MCCLENDON, CONSTABLE FOR BLEDSOE COUNTY,
$4,000.00...SECURITIES: PETER HOODENPYLE, WILLIAM BROWN, WILLIAM
M. ORME

BOND OF B. F. BRIDGMAN, ELECTED RANGER FOR BLEDSOE
COUNTY...$500.00...SECURITIES: GEORGE OXSHER AND BURREL LEA

THIS DAY JOHN M. BRIDGMAN CAME INTO OPEN COURT AND WAS DULY SWORN
IN AS DEPT. REGISTER

P. 448   JUNE TERM 1846

PRESENT ON THE BENCH: THE WORSHIPFUL JONATHAN WHITESIDE

THIS DAY THOMAS SWAFFORD RETURNED IN OPEN COURT HIS ROAD ORDER AS
OVERSEER

JOHN THURMAN PRODUCED IN OPEN COURT THREE WOLF SCALPS, WOLVES
KILLED IN BLEDSOE COUNTY, NOT OVER FOUR MONTHS OLD

THIS DAY MARTIN A. SMITH PRESENTED IN COURT HIS RESIGNATION AS
JUSTICE OF THE PEACE...ORDERED RECORDED

THIS DAY WILLIAM RECTOR PRESENTED IN OPEN COURT HIS ORDER AS
OVERSEER

(NOTE OF TYPIST OF THE WPA TRANSCRIPT: THE FOLLOWING BOND WAS
MARKED OUT IN ORIGINAL BOOK WITH A BIG X.)...BOND OF JOHN PARHAM,
APPOINTED ADMINISTRATOR OF (NAME NOT
GIVEN)...$3,000.00...SECURITIES: WILLIAM STEPHENS AND A. M.
ANDERSON...NOT SIGNED

WEST WALKER APPOINTED OVERSEER OF ROAD IN ROOM AND STEAD OF C. C.
STRANAHAN...JOHN PARHAM, APPOINTED OVERSEER IN ROOM OF WILLIAM
RECTOR...WILLIAM CLARK, APPOINTED OVERSEER IN ROOM OF THOS.
SWAFFORD

BOND OF JOHN PARHAM, ADMINISTRATOR OF ESTATE OF JOHN PARHAM,
DECEASED...$3,000.00 ...SECURITIES: WILLIAM STEPHENS AND AUDLEY
M. ANDERSON

P. 453 ORDERED THAT ISAAC STEPHENS, JAMES ORME, WILLIAM NAIL BE
APPOINTED...ONE YEARS PROVISION FOR DORY PARHAM, THE WIDOW OF
JOHNSON PARHAM, DECD...MAKE REPORT NEXT TERM

P. 454   JULY SESSION 1846

PRESENT ON THE BENCH: THE WORSHIPFUL JONATHAN WHITESIDE, SAMUEL
RANKIN, HUNTER, HIXSON, BRYANT, SHERRILL, BROWN

JOHN THURMAN PRODUCED IN OPEN COURT THREE WOLF SCALPS...SAID
WOLVES WERE KILLED IN BLEDSOE COUNTY, NOT OVER FOUR MONTHS OLD

O. P. SCHOOLFIELD APPOINTED OVERSEER OF ROAD THAT RUNS THRUE HIS
FARM...TO WORK THE ROAD WITH HIS OWN HANDS

GEORGE OXSHER APPOINTED OVERSEER OF ROAD JAS. A. THURMANS TO
SPRINGS ROAD, WITH THE HANDS ON HALES PLACE AND COLBERT AND JOHN
WILLOUGHBY HAND IN SCHOOLFIELDS PLACE

BOND OF WILLIAM WALKER, COUNTY TRUSTEE, $2,000.00...SECURITIES: JOHN BRIDGMAN AND E. H. BOYD...ACCOUNTS OF COMMON SCHOOL FUND FROM STATE OF TENNESSEE

ALLEN MERIMAN APPOINTED OVERSEER OF ROAD FROM SPRING & ROAD DOWN TO PHELPS, WITH THE HANDS THAT LIVES ON JAS. ROBERSONS LAND AND THE HANDS ON THIS SIDE CREEK, ALSO THE HANDS THAT FORMERLY WORK ON SAID ROAD FROM MERRIMANS DOWN

THOS. R. ROGERS APPOINTED OVERSEER OF ROAD LEADING FROM THE TOWN BRIDGE TO ARON SWAFFORD BRANCH IN ROOM AND STEAD OF ARON SWAFFORD

J. M. BOYD APPOINTED OVERSEER OF ROAD COMMENCING AT ALEXANDER LAMBS SPRING BRANCH AND WORK TO THE CREK WHAR ALBERT PHELPS NOW LIVES IN THE ROOM OF C. LAMB

ORDERED THAT ISAAC ROBERSONS ROAD AND HANDS ON THE EAST SIDE OF THE RIVER BE PUT UNDER JACOB KEEDY

ORDERED THAT MARTIN HARDEN BE RELEASED FROM PAYING A POLE TAX

ORDERED THAT ALFRED M. SKILLERN HAVE FOLLOWING HANDS ATTACHED TO HIS ROAD: G. W. CETCHAM, CHARLES CETCHAM, JOHN ?GOURIN, JOHN FAIRBANKS, HIRAM BEDWELL, E. M. MCLAUGHLIN

ORDERED THAT D. F. COCKE BE RELEASED FROM PAYING TAX ON MOUNTAIN LAND WHICH WAS VALUED AT TWO THOUSAND DOLLARS AND HE IS RELEASED BY THE COURT TO FIVE DOLLARS

SAMUEL W. ROBERSON APPOINTED OVERSEER OF ROAD LEADING FROM BOWMANS BY WAY OF HIS MILL...TO KEEP UP ROAD WITH HIS OWN HANDS

JURY OF VIEW: JOSEPH NEWMAN, RALPH SCOTT, CRAVIN SHEARL, JOHN D. MORRIS, JOHN F. GREER, WM. RENFROW, GEORGE DAWSON...TO VIEW ROAD LEADING FROM SHERILS GAP TO INTERSECT GORDONS ROAD NEAR JAMES M. REVIS WHICH ROAD WILLIAM RENFROW IS OVERSEER, SO AS TO LEAVE OUT THAT PART WHAR HUGH MILLER PATTON NOW LIVING

ALEXANDER H. MONTGOMERY HAS DEPARTED THIS LIFE...IN HIS WILL HE APPOINTED THOS. N. FRAZIER AND JAMES A. TULLOSS HIS EXECUTORS...SAME DULY PROVEN BEFORE SAID COURT, ORDERD TO BE RECORDED

WILLIAM NEWBY, AN ORPHAN OF AGE OF ELEVEN YEARS OLD, BOUND TO
EDWIN BEATTY...AGREEMENT...HUGH BEATTY, SECURITY

P. 460   BOND OF WILLIAM WALKER, COUNTY TRUSEE,
$2,000.00...SECURITIES: JOHN BRIDGMAN AND E. H. BOYD...

P. 461   AUGUST SESSION   1846

PRESENT ON THE BENCH: THE WORSHIPFUL JONATHAN RANKIN BROWN LODEN
BILLINGSLEY

JOHN BILLINGSLEY, COMMISSIONED JUSTICE OF THE PEACE FOR BLEDSOE
COUNTY, CAME INTO COURT, TOOK OATHS, TOOK HIS SEAT ON THE BENCH

JOHN F. GREER PRESENTED IN OPEN COURT HIS RESIGNATION AS JUSTICE
OF THE PEACE FOR BLEDSOE COUNTY

JOHN FORD PRODUCED IN OPEN COURT 8 WOLF SCALPS...WOLVES KILLED IN
BLEDSOE COUNTY, WERE NOT THOUGHT TO BE OVER FOUR MONTHS OLD

FOLLOWING NAMED GENTLEMEN TO BE SUMMONED AS JURORS AT NOVEMBER
TERM OF CIRCUIT COURT 1846:
1ST DIST.   MARTIN BROYLES, ROBERT A. RENFROE
2   D   JAMES GIBSON, DANIEL BROWN
3   DIST. CRAVEN SHERILL, GEORGE JONES, GREEN B. SELBY
4   D   WILLIAM MOSS, JOSEPH MCDOWEL
5.   WILLIAM S. BROWN, ISAM HALE, WILLIAM FARMER
6.   ISAAC B. HENSON, WILLIAM S. HUNTER, S, D, BRIDGMAN,
            PETER HOODENPYLE
7,   THOS. FOSTER, GEORGE OXSHER
8.   D.   ISAAC ROBERSON, OWIN BRYANT
9   DIST. JAMES HIXSON, RIGHT JOHNSON
10.   J. R. WHEELER, JACOB TETARS, ROBERT OWINS
CONSTABLE B. R. SMITH, E. H. BOYD

ALLEN L. PITTS APPOINTED OVERSEER OF ROAD IN ROOM AND STEAD OF
CALVIN J. MCDONOUGH

BURREL LEA AND _____ THE WRITTEN WITNESS TO THE LAST WILL AND
TESTIMONY OF JOHN COOK DECEASED AFTER BEING DULY SWORN AN OATH
ACKNOWLEDGED THE WILL TO BE J___ (BLANK) AND THE FACTOR THEREIN
CONTAINED.

P. 464   BOND OF SHIILOH OWEN AND BURREL LEA, EXECUTORS OF WILL

OF JOHN COOK, DECEASED...$1,000.00

P. 466   SEPTEMBER SESSION   1846

PRESENT ON THE EBNCH: THE WORSHIPFUL JONATHAN WHITESIDE, SAMUEL
RANKIN, WILLIAM FOSTER

WILLIAM SKILLERN APPOINTED OVERSEER OF ROAD IN ROOM OF S UEL
VERNON

WILLIAM RUSH, COMMISSIONED JUSTICE OF THE PEACE FOR BLEDSOE
COUNTY, TOOK OATHS, TOOK HIS SEAT N THE BENCH

BOND OF WILLIAM SKILERN, ADMINISTRATOR OF ESTATE OF JOHN SKILLER,
DECEASED...$500.00...SECURITY: A. A. SKILLERN...NOT SIGNED

P. 469 BOND OF DANIEL WHITE, ELECTED CONSTABLE FOR BLEDSOE
COUNTY...$4,000.00...SECURITIES: JOHN BRIDGMAN AND A. M.
ANDERSON...

BOND OF WILLIAM SKILLERN, ADMINISTRATOR OF ESTATE OF JOHN
SKILLERN, DECEASED...$500.00...SECURITIES: A. A. SKILLERN, JAS.
A. TULLOSS, A, M, ANDERSON

P. 472   OCTOBER SESION   1846

PRESENT ON THE BENCH: THE WORSHIPFUL JONATHAN WHITESIDE, WILLIAM
STEPHENS, SAMUEL H. HUNTER, JOHN BILLINGSLEY, HENRY SHEAREL,
WILLIAM BROWN, HUTCHESON CARMACK HEARD FOSTER

ARON SWAFFORD APPOINTED OVERSEER OF ROAD IN ROOM AND STEAD OF
SAMUEL GOTT

ALLOWANCE OF $12.75 TO JOHN B. MURPHY FOR SERVICE RENDERED IN
SUPPLYING THE COURT HOUSE AND FURNISHING WOOD FROM 1 JANY 46 TO
OCT. 1 46

P. 473 ALLOWANCE OF FOURTY CENTS TO WILLIAM P. HUNTER FOR PUTING
IN A LABERDOR IN THE COURT HOUSE...ALLOWANCE OF $35.00 TO S. C.
NORWOOD FOR KEEPING WILLIS IVY IN BLEDSOE COUNTY JAIL FROM 27TH
MAY 1846 TO 23RD AUG. 46

ALLOWANCE TO JOHN THURMAN...$1.50 FOR FURNISHING ONE STOCK LOCK
FOR THE COURT HOUSE

THE VOTE BEING TAKEN THAT THE SHERIFF PAY TO J. J. P. THE TAX ON
FOUR HUNDRED DOLLARS WORTH OF PROPERTY...AFFIRMED IN THE
AFFIRMATIVE

P. 474 ALLOWANCE OF SEVENTY FIVE CENTS TO BRIDGMAN & HICKS FOR
FINDING 3 PAR OF BOOTS

JURY OF VIEW: ISAAC STEPHENS, JAMES HOLDERMAN, PLEASANT BREWER,
BIRD BREWER, GEORGE PRESLEY...TO VIEW OUT A ROAD FROM STEPHENS TO
LOWERYS BEGINNING AT THE CORNER OF JOEL HALLS FIELD AND BY HIS
HOUSE SO AS TO INTERSECT THE OLD ROAD NEAR A POND DISTANCE ONE
QUARTER OF A MILE

S. C. NORWOOD APPOINTED TO SUPERINTEND IN HAVING JAIL WINDOWS
ENCLOSED FOR THE SAFEKEEPING OF THE PRISONERS

FOLLOWING GENTLEMEN APPOINTED TO LAY OFF A ROAD BEGINNING AT THE
VAN BUREN LINE ON CUMBERLAND MOUNTAIN TO INTERSECT THOMAS
GARDNERS TURNPIKE ROAD AT THE TOP OF THE MOUNTAIN: HIRAM
BEDWELL, JAMES COWIN, THOMAS SUTHERLAND, THOMAS FOSTER, ISAAC
HUMBLE

BOND OF DAVID NORRIS, $30.00...SECURITIES: WILLIAM M. ORME AND
SAMUEL RANKIN...ADMINISTRATOR OF ESTATE OF ABOVE NORRIS (NOT
GIVEN)

SMITH MERRIMAN RELEASED OF PAYING TAX ON FOUR HUNDRED ACRES OF
LAND VALUED AT ONE HUNDRED DOLLARS

ORDERED THAT THE SHERIFF.TAKE CHARLES TOMPSON A PAUPER INSAIN
FOURTH WITH TO LUNATICK HOSPITAL IN THE CITY OF NASHVILLE

BOND OF RUSSEL GOTT, EXECUTOR OF ESTATE OF SAMUEL GOTT,
DECEASED...$500.00...SECURITY: BUREL LEA

JURY OF VIEW: NATHANIEL BROYLES, WILLIAM HEDGECOTH, JAMES
HEDGECOTH, BAZEL HEDGECOTH, WILLIAM KENTON, ROBERT BURK, ELIJAH
HALEY AND PETER HOODENPYLE...TO MARK OUT ROAD OF FIRST CLASS
LEADING FROM THE CRAB ORCHARD AT OR NEAR THEAR TO ENTER STAGE
ROAD AT OR NEAR NATH BROYLES OR CHARLES LOWERYS...REPORT NEXT
TERM

ORDERED THAT THE PUBLIC ROAD LEADING FROM SAMUEL WORTHINGTONS TO
HU BATTYS BE DISENLED AND THAT WILLIAM CLARK, S. J. SHEARLEY,
JOHN SWAFFORD AND THE WIDOW SWAFFORDS HANDS , JAMES BILLINGSLEY
AND JOHN BILLINGSLEY HANDS TO WORK UNDER CLATEN GREER, AND THE
HANDS LIVING AT CHARLES CLARKS AND SAMUEL WORTHINGTONS HANDS WORK
UNDER JONATHAN CLARK AND SAID CLARK ROAD TO BE CONTINUED AS FAR
DOWN AS JOHN BILLINGSLEYS BRANCH

RUSSEL GOOT (GOTT) PRESENTED IN OPEN COURT THE LAST WILL AND
TESTIMONY OF SAMUEL GOOT (GOTT) DECEASED WHICH WAS PROVEN BY
BURREL LEA AND GEORGE JONES SUBSCRIBED WITNESSES THERETO...SAID
GOOT ENTERED INTO BOND...ORDER TO BE SPREAD ON RECORD

DAVID NORRIS WAS APPOINTED ADMINISTRATOR OF THE ESTATE OF ARON
NORRIS DECEASED...ENTERED INTO BOND

                              THE COURT APPOINTED SAMUEL H.
HUNTER CHAIRMAN PROTEM

P. 481   NOVEMBER SESSION   1846

PRESENT ON THE BENCH: THE WORSHIPFUL JONATHAN WHITESIDE, WILLIAM
BROWN BILLINGSLEY STEPHENS

WILLIAM SKILLERN, EXECUTOR OF ESTATE OF JOHN SKILLERN DECEASED
RETURNED INTO OPEN COURT THE INVENTORY OF ALL THE PERSONAL
PROPERTY OF SAID ESTATE

WILLY AND ALLEN MERRIMAN, EXECUTORS OF ESTATE OF MARKUS MERRIMAN,
RETURNED IN OPEN COURT AN INVENTORY OF ALL THE SLAVES OF THE SAID
DECD.

ORDERED THAT THE SHERIFF BRING BEFORE THE NEXT COUNTY COURT
JULYAN FOSTER THREE OLDEST CHILDRES AS THE LAW DIRECTS

JOHN PARHAM, EXECUTOR OF ESTATE OF JOHN PARHAM SENR. DECEASED
RETURNED IN OPEN COURT THE INVENTORY OF THE SAILS OF THE PERSONAL
PROPERTY OF THE DECD

COUNTY

RECEIVED PIKEVILLE OCT. 15 1846 OF THOMAS W. HALE CLERK
$46 10/100 THE COUNTY REVINEW DUE FROM HIM TO THE TREASURER OF
BLEDSOE COUNTY...S/WM. WALKER, TREASURER OF BLEDSOE COUNTY

$225 69/100   NASHVILLE   NOV. 20TH 1846   NO. 3246
RECEIVED OF WM. ORME TWO HUNDRED AND TWENTY FIVE DOLLARS AND
SIXTY NINE CENTS AUDITED TO HIM BY NO. 3246. AND DUE ON ACCOUNTOF
REVINEW BY HIM COLLECTED AS CLERK OF BLEDSOE COUNTY FROM 1_ SEPT
1845 TO THE 6 OF APR. 1846
(SIGNED DUPLICATE)   R. B. TURNER
                                          TREASURER TENNESSEE

FOLLOWING NAMED JUSTICE OF PEACE APPOINTED REVINEW COMMISSIONERS
FOR THE YEAR 1847 TO TAKE A LIST OF TAXABLE PROPERTY AND POLL:WM.
RUSH, 1ST...JAMES WALKER, 2ND...HENRY SHERRILL, 3RD...WM. BROWN,
4TH...JOHN BILLINGSLEY, 5TH...WM. STEPHENS, 6TH...E. M. HALE,
7TH...JESSEY CARMACK, 8TH...JOSEPH HIXSON, 9TH...JOEL WHEELER
WITH ____ (BLANK)

NOTE: A BOND IS PARTIALLY RECORDED: WE BENJAMIN BRIANT
GEORGEOXSHEER OWEN BRYANT & ISAAC ROBERSON ARE HELD AND FIRMLY
BOUND UNTO JONATHAN WHITESIDE CHAIRMAN OF THE COUNTY COURT OF
BLEDSOE COUNTY AFORESAID AND HIS SUCCESSORS IN OFFICE IN THE
PENAL SUM OF ONE THOUSAND DOLLARS

ORDER THAT JOHN REAL PAY COST OF THIS SUIT IN HIS BEHALF...HAS
UNTILL NEXT TERM TO PAY SAME OR BE SUBJECT TO RESPONDENT FOR THIS
OFFENCE

RUSSEL GAULT EXECUTOR OF ESTATE OF SAMUEL GAUT DECEASED HAS
UNTILL NEXT TERM TO RETURN FULL INVENTORY OF PROPERTY OF SAID
DECEASED

FOLLOWING GENTLEMEN APPOINTED JURORS FOR THE NEXT TERM OF CIRCUIT
COURT FOR BLEDSOE COUNTY: CHATTEN T. POLLARD, GEORGE DAWSON,
WETHERSTON S. GREER, JOHN FORD, SR., WM. KERLEY, ROBERT LEA,
C. K. SHERILL, J. G. M. WOODS, JOEL SEAGRAVES, J. J. POPE, ARON
SWAFFORD, A. B. BILLINGSLEY, JAS. SKILLERN, J. G. COKE, A. P.
GREEN, JOSPEH PANE, WILLIAM A SCHOOLFIELD, WM. SMITH, ISAAC
ANDERSON, A. H. NAIL, LAFAYETTE WILLIAMSON, H. LASETER, H. HORN.
R. RUSSEL, J. MCWILLIAMS...AND E. L. L. BOYD AND WM. DAY
CONSTABLES TO WAIT ON COURT

BENJ. BRYANT, GUARDIAN FOR MINOR HEIRS OF J. A. MILLARD...AFTER

DUE CONSIDERATION IT IS CONSIDERED BY THE COURT THAT HE EXECUTE
HIS BOND AT NEXT TERM OF COURT

ORDERED THAT WILLIAM SMITH BE RELEASED FROM PAYING AMT. OF $.12
THAT BEING THE AMOUNT WHICH IS RESPECTFULLY CHARGED TO SMITH

ORDERED THAT ISAAH GREER BE APPOINTED OVERSEER OF ROAD FROM WHERF
IT TURNS THE VALLEY ROAD WITH THE SAME HANDS AND BOUNDS THAT
WILLIAM THOMAS HAD

JOHN HALL APPOINTED OVERSEER OF ROAD IN ROOM AND STEAD OF WM.
RIGSBY

THIS DAY PERSONALY APPEARED IN OPEN COURT WILLIAM MERRIMAN AND
PROVED BY HIS OWN OATH AN ACCOUNT AGAINST THE ESTATE OF MARK
MERRIMAN DEC. FOR THE FOLLOWING AMT...$543.76

WPA TRANSCRIBER'S NOTE: PAGES 493 TO 528 IN THE ORIGINAL BOOK
ARE BLANK

P. 528

STATE OF TENNESSEE   )
)   KNOW ALL MEN BY THESE PRESENTS THAT WE
)   THOMAS J. SHERLEY WILLIAM STEPHENS
BLEDOSE COUNTY   )   ARE HELD AND FIRMLY BOUND UNTO _____
IN THE PENAL SUM OF $1,000.00 TO BE LEVIED OF ALL GOODS AND
CHATTLES LANDS AND TENEMENTS BUT TO BE VOID ON CONDITION THAT J.
THOMAS J. SHERLEY SHALL WELL AND TRULY FAITHFULLY PERFORM ALL THE
DUTIES BELONGING TO AND INVOLVING ON ME AS SUPERINTENDENT OF THE
P'OOR HOUSE THEN THIS OBLIGATION TO BE VOID OTHERWISE TO REMAIN IN
FULL FORCE AND VIRTUE...(NOT SIGNED)

THE END

COUNTY COURT MINUTES
BLEDSOE COUNTY
1841 -1846

AREL   64
ARLE   81
ACUFF   12, 13, 18, 34, 37, 40, 45, 54, 58, 65, 73, 74, 81,
                82
AKING   66
ALLEN   1, 11, 14, 49, 74, 86
ALSISON   64
ANDERSON   2, 6, 7, 8, 9, 12, 13, 15, 22, 28, 37, 38, 44, 45,
                46, 53, 56, 58, 63, 66, 68, 75, 82, 83, 86, 91, 94,
                97
ARMS   12
AUSTIN   73, 79, 8L, 82
AUSTON   2
BAITY   16, 17, 26, 36, 38, 67
BALLARD   78
BARGER   2, 24
BARKER   57
BARNETT   8, 10, 64
BARNETTE   64
BATTY   96
BAYER   64
BEACH   42, 57
BEALLEN   75
BEATTE   42
BEATTY   1, 2, 3, 4, 5, 7, 8, 10, 12, 13, 14, 15, 17, 20,
                20, 22, 26, 65, 67, 74, 93
REDWELL   92
BILLINGSLEY   2, 3, 4, 6, 8, 9, 10, 11, 12, 13, 14, 18, 25, 30,
                32, 33, 38, 42, 43, 45, 51, 60, 67, 73, 80, 82, 88,
                93, 94, 96, 97
BLALOCK   64
BLAYLOCK   8, 50, 86
BOLING   70
BOLTON   80
BOMIN   18
BOULDIN   17
BOWMAN   64, 66, 85, 88, 92
BOYD   12, 17, 22, 23, 30, 32, 34, 37, 42, 44, 50, 51, 52,
                53, 60, 64, 68, 77, 79, 86, 92, 93, 97
BRADFORD   12
BREWER   64, 95
BRIANT   15, 19, 22, 24, 25, 26, 31, 33, 36, 37, 39, 44, 45,
                45, 51, 52, 55, 56, 57, 58, 59, 60, 66, 68, 74, 97
BRIDGEMAN   34
BRIDGMAN   3, 4, 13, 16, 31, 32, 34, 42, 44, 47, 48, 51, 53,
                55, 60, 62, 66, 68, 69, 70, 75, 79, 85, 87, 90, 92,
                92, 93, 94, 95
BRISTOE   22
BRISTOL   67, 70, 73

```
BRISTOW          85
BROCK            18
BROWN             1,  2,  3,  4,  5,  6,  7,  8,  9,  10,  11,  12,  13,  14,  16,
                 17, 18, 21, 22, 24, 25, 26, 27, 28, 30, 31, 32, 33,
                 33, 34, 35, 36, 37, 39, 40, 41, 43, 44, 45, 47, 50,
                 51, 53, 54, 56, 58, 59, 60, 61, 62, 63, 65, 67, 68,
                 68, 69, 70, 71, 72, 73, 74, 75, 77, 79, 80, 86, 87,
                 88, 89, 90, 91
BROYLES          93
BRYANT           32, 78, 79, 80, 86, 87, 89, 91, 93, 97
BURCH            82
BURDITT          64
BURK             95
BURKE            55, 72, 86
BURNETT          23
BUSELL           36

CAMPBELL          8, 64
CANADA           18
CANTRELL          3
CARDER            5,  6, 12, 13, 22, 30, 32, 39, 44, 56, 74, 86
CARMACK          54, 85, 94, 97
CARNAHAN         81
CARNES           22, 29, 45, 46, 49, 51, 60, 67, 84
CARTER           15, 28, 38, 64
CATCHUM           3
CETCHAM          92
CHAMBERS          8
CHRISTIAN        82
CLARK            13, 21, 25, 43, 49, 55, 58, 69, 76, 91, 96
CLEMONS           2
CLOSE            38
CLOUD             3
COCKE             7, 87, 88, 92
COKE             97
COLBERT          40, 52, 91
COLEMAN           3
COLVARD          59, 60
CONDREY          74
CONLEY            8, 23, 72
CONLY            41
COOK              3, 34, 39, 40, 41, 58, 93, 94
COOKE            30
COULSTON         16, 19, 56
COULTER           1,  2, 11, 12, 14, 16, 18, 37, 38, 41, 49, 53, 58,
                 60, 64, 65, 67, 73, 76, 84, 85
COWAN            40
COWIN            95
COX              21, 37, 89
COZZATT          82
CRAWFORD          6, 44, 45, 47, 56, 65, 75
CROZIER           9, 14, 39, 56,57, 67, 83, 90
CRUTCHFIELD       4,  7,  8, 20, 52
CURTIS           21, 73
```

```
CUZZART           64


DALTON            3,  5,  10,  12,  20,  34,  41,  52,  53,  74,  81
DANIEL           56
DAVENPORT        65
DAVIS            16,  54,  74,  82
DAWSON            5,  13,  22,  26,  28,  31,  32,  33,  34,  38,  40,  50,  51,
                 54,  56,  58,  60,  65,  70,  71,  72,  74,  79,  86,  87,  90,
                 92,  97
DAY              36,  76,  86,  88,  97
DENTON           11
DEVENPORT        25,  69,  71
DORIS            10
DORSEY           13,  33,  37,  45,  46,  86
DORSY            25
DORTON           10,  77,  86,  89
DOTSON            3
GREGGIN           3
DUGER             3
DUGGER            8
DUSSEE            3
DWIGGINS         12,  33,  34,  40,  43,  53,  63


EDWARD            3
ELLISON          89
ENGLISH          83
EPERSON           2,  3
EVANS            44,  58,  67,  72,  90
EVINS            92
EVITT            72
EWTON             2,  24


FAIRBANKS        92
FAN              50
FANN             44,  61
FARA             49
FARE             39
FARMER            5,  26,  39,  62,  67,  71,  77,  86,  93
FARR             40,  48
FARRAR           77
FERGUSON         34
FINLEY            6,  18,  43
FIRBUSH           6
FORD             38,  57,  58,  74,  93,  97
FOSTER            1,  3,  5,  7,  12,  13,  14,  15,  17,  19,  20,  22,  23,
                 24,  25,  26,  27,  28,  30,  31,  32,  33,  34,  36,  37,  38,
                 40,  41,  42,  43,  44,  45,  46,  47,  48,  50,  51,  54,  56,
                 57,  61,  62,  65,  66,  67,  68,  69,  70,  75,  77,  79,  80,
                 81,  86,  87,  93,  94,  95,  96
FRAILEY          49
FRANKLIN         20
```

```
FRAZIER          70, 71, 82, 85, 89, 92
FREEMAN          80
FREMAN            3, 64
FULKINS          64


GALT             81
GANAWAY           6, 73
GARDNER          53, 95
GAUT             97
GENTRY           36, 56
GIBSON           50, 58, 93
GILBREATH        62, 72
GILBRETH         82
GIPSON           36, 38, 44, 45, 51, 73
GLENTWORTH       36
GODSEY            3
GOFF              3
GOOT             96
GORDON           25, 56, 70, 72, 73, 86, 92
GOTT             12, 94, 95, 96
GOURIN (?)       92
GRAHAM            7, 42, 56, 64, 67, 72, 88
GRASON           11
GREEN             3, 16, 19, 20, 36, 38, 45, 46, 47, 55, 56, 57, 61,
                 65, 71, 75, 87, 97
GREER             1, 4, 5, 7, 8, 9, 11, 12, 13, 14, 19, 22, 24, 25,
                 26, 28, 29, 31, 32, 33, 34, 37, 38, 40, 43, 44, 50,
                 51, 55, 56, 58, 60, 61, 62, 65, 67, 68, 69, 70, 71,
                 72, 79, 81, 85, 87, 89, 92, 93, 96, 97, 98
GRIMES           77
GUALT            89


HAIL             18, 53, 85
HALE              3, 13, 18, 32, 35, 36, 41, 43, 44, 46, 49, 50, 51,
                 52, 58, 59, 60, 66,67, 68, 70, 72, 74, 75, 76, 80,
                 81, 82, 86, 87, 88, 91, 93, 97
HALEY            55, 74, 86, 95
HALL              8, 14, 18, 22, 46, 82, 95, 98
HAMBLE           28, 42
HAMILTON         25, 41, 60, 77, 89
HANEY             3
HANKENS          76
HANKINS           8, 29
HARDEN           92
HARDIN           64
HARRIS           13, 20, 65, 86, 88
HARRISON          3, 18, 42, 53
HASKEW           14, 19, 40, 66, 67, 68, 72, 88, 89
HAY              33
HEARD             5, 6, 8, 13, 22, 47, 63, 79, 83, 94
HEDGCOTH          8, 20, 38, 55
HEDGECOTH        14, 15, 20, 33, 55, 67, 72, 73, 86, 95
```

```
HELTON              82
HENDERSON           36, 56
HENEGAR             50
HENNIGAR             6, 9
HENNIGER            74
HENRY               76
HENSON               4, 9, 25, 29, 37,38, 58, 60, 63, 71, 93
HERD                21, 24, 25, 26, 28, 32, 36, 40, 45, 48, 49, 51, 52,
                    54, 62, 68, 75, 86
HICKENBOTTOM        40
HICKENBOTTUM        14
HICKS                7, 12, 24, 47, 48,55, 61, 77, 82, 85, 87, 95
HICKSON              2, 5, 10
HIDER               18, 58, 64, 78
HINCH               24, 31, 46, 52, 67, 71
HINES               33
HIXSON               1, 4, 5, 7, 10, 13, 14, 15, 16, 19, 21, 22, 24,
                    25, 26, 30, 31, 33, 35, 36, 38, 40, 44, 45, 50, 52,
                    54, 56, 57, 59, 60, 65, 66, 68,  70, 73, 74, 77,
                    80, 84, 85, 86, 89, 91, 93, 97
HOGE                34
HOLDEN              10, 72
HOLDEN               3
HOLDERMAN           95
HOLEMAN             46, 66
HOLLAND              3
HOLLOWAY            89
HOLMAN              73
HOODENPYL           29, 35, 38, 39, 68, 69,83, 86, 90
HOODENPYLE           5, 6, 7, 29, 42, 86, 90, 93, 95
HOOTS                2, 21, 24
HOPKINS              2
HORN                 3, 7, 10, 14, 23, 27, 40, 42, 49, 63, 85, 97
HOWARD               3, 5, 22, 51, 52, 55, 75
HOWL                47
HOYEL               30
HUGHES              42
HUGHS               10, 30, 34, 42, 54, 56, 58, 65, 67, 72, 73, 77, 79,
                    84, 89
HUMBLE              42, 51, 57, 86, 88, 95
HUNTER              13, 15, 17, 22, 24, 25, 26, 27, 30, 31, 37, 40, 41,
                    44, 45, 48, 50, 51, 52, 53, 54, 61, 65, 66, 69, 70,
                    73, 74, 75, 76, 77, 78, 79, 80, 81, 84, 86, 87, 91,
                    93, 94, 96
HUTCHESON           11, 25, 26, 27, 31, 37, 41, 44, 45, 46, 50, 51, 56,
                    60, 61, 62, 67, 69, 70, 75, 79, 80, 81, 82, 84, 86,
                    87, 89, 94


INGRAM               1, 5, 11, 46, 67, 89
IVITT                8
IVY                 56, 57, 71, 94
```

```
JAMES          3
JENTRY         15
JOHNSON         6, 7, 13, 14, 17, 28, 34, 37, 40, 46, 57, 58, 62,
               70, 79, 80, 93
JONES           2, 3, 9, 24, 41, 52, 74, 77, 78, 93, 96
JONSON         56
JOURDAN        57
JOURDEN        56
JOYS           68


KEARLY          4, 59
KEASY          27
KEEDY           5, 17, 20, 21, 38, 39, 40, 52, 57, 68, 73, 92
KEENER          1, 10
KELLY          23, 29
KELTNER        75
KENNY          23
KENTON         95
KERLEY         35, 45, 46, 50, 73, 89, 97
KERLY           4, 3L, 35, 45, 60, 82
KERSY          26
KERTIS         39, 53
KILGORE        11
KIME           31
KIMME          31
KIMMER          2, 31, 33, 34, 36, 69
KINSY          26
KINZY           3
KIRKLIN         5, 13, 17, 22, 38, 45, 50, 61, 70
KNIGHT         11, 64
KNON   (?)     86
KNOX           13


LACESETER      30, 37, 39, 44, 60
LADEN          34
LAMB            4, 5, 11, 15, 22, 37,50, 58, 89, 92
LAMBRETH       15
LANGLEY        90
LASETER        10, 42, 74, 77, 97
LASITER        73, 79, 85
LAY            62
LEA             4, 5, 6, 7, 8, 9, 10, 11, 12, 14, 21, 41, 76, 77,
               83, 86, 88, 89, 90, 93, 95, 96, 97
LEE             1, 2, 3, 19, 25, 34, 40, 47, 56, 61, 62, 66, 67,
               74
LEWIS          63
LIVELY         89
LLOYD          30, 34, 42, 44, 53, 58, 66, 68, 79, 86, 87
LODEN          70, 71, 88, 93
LOOING         24
LOONY           3
```

```
LOVE              3
LOVING            6
LOWDEN            9, 25, 56, 69, 72, 80, 85
LOWE              5, 35, 87
LOWERY            14, 22, 25, 28, 33, 40, 43, 46, 49, 56, 57, 64, 66,
                  69, 73, 79, 90, 95
LOWRY             44
LOYD              5, 6, 7, 22, 28, 73


MAGERS            31
MANFEE            61
MANGU             48, 51
MANING            31
MANNING           26
MANNON            76
MANOR             29
MANSFIELD         3, 21, 23, 24
MANZER            18
MARLOW            56, 64
MASSE             57, 58
MASSEE            22, 39, 58
MASSEY            68
MASSIE            74
MASSY             1
MATHISS           30, 57
MATTHESS          56
MATTHEWS          2
MAUGE             39, 40
MAUSSE            37
MAUZEE            51
MAUZY             13, 70, 71, 85
MAYERS            29
MEREMAN           78
MERIMAN           56, 92
MERRIMAN          18, 42, 52, 66, 77, 92, 95, 96, 98
MEYERS            78
MILLARD           2, 18, 60, 63, 66, 97
MILLER            3, 38, 42, 47, 57, 59, 73, 81, 84
MIRES             14
MITTS             56, 60
MOIS              24
MONTGOMERY        38, 61, 85, 89, 92
MOONEYHAM         64
MOONYHAM          3, 54
MOORE             3, 6, 19
MORRIS            40, 41, 49, 69, 72, 74, 92
MOSS              14, 64, 93
MOYERS            8, 58
MOYRES            58, 64, 74
MOYSES            43, 64
MUNCY             25, 49
MURPHY            55, 61, 66, 73, 83, 90, 94
MYERS             64
```

```
MCCALL           18
MCCARROLL        80
MCCAUL            7
MCCLAIN          55
MCCLENAHAN       67
MCCLENDEN        44, 51, 65, 68, 70, 71, 72
MCCLENDON         8, 13, 14, 15, 20, 26, 28, 34, 90
MCCLINE           3
MCCULEY          30
MCCULLY           8
MCCULY           30
MCDONOUGH         6, 51, 58, 64, 70, 90, 93
MCDOWEL          22, 34, 38, 56, 58, 59, 67, 78, 93
MCDOWELL          5, 8, 42, 51, 73, 76
MCLAUGHLIN       92
MCNABB           82
MCNEW            56
MCREYNOLDS       11, 29, 40, 48, 51, 58, 79, 86
MCVAY             2
MCWILLIAMS       10, 17, 58, 67, 85, 97


NAIL             38, 58, 72, 91, 97
NANEY             3
NANNY             4, 6, 12, 13, 23, 44, 55, 61, 62
NARAMORE          7, 58
NARRAMORE        38
NAVISS           25
NAY              25
NELSON            1, 12, 13, 25
NESBIT            6
NEWBE            25
NEWBEE           28
NEWBY             5, 53, 93
NEWMAN            2, 5, 20, 28, 35, 56, 71, 75, 92
NICHOL           78
NICHOLS          39, 55, 58, 64, 66, 67
NORRIS           95
NORWOOD           6, 59, 66, 67, 73, 74, 75, 80, 88, 94, 95


OFFESERS         20
OGLE             64
ONEIL            16, 17, 18, 36, 54
ONIEL            15
ORME              5, 9, 10, 11, 12, 13, 14, 15, 22, 24, 25, 26, 27,
                 28, 31, 32, 33, 35, 37, 40, 41, 42, 44, 45, 46, 48,
                 49, 50, 51, 52, 53, 54, 56, 57, 58, 59, 60, 61, 62,
                 63, 65, 66, 68, 69, 70, 71, 72, 73, 78, 79, 83, 87,
                 89, 90, 91, 95, 97
ORMES            13, 21
OWEN             93
OWENS             5, 6, 9, 32, 44, 46, 62, 67, 83, 89
```

```
OWINS          93
OXIER          27, 71
OXSHEER        11, 16, 51, 57, 58, 59, 72, 73, 77, 78, 82, 83, 88,
               97
OXSHER          9, 28, 35, 42, 43, 48, 49, 59, 86, 90, 91, 93


PAINE           7, 13, 32, 38, 50, 51, 56, 66, 67, 70, 76
PANE           97
PANKEY         20, 74, 86
PANNELL        82
PANTHER        56
PARHAM          2, 90
PARKER         14
PARKS          64
PARSON         55
PATTON          2, 34, 46, 52, 76, 78, 89, 92
PAYNE          12, 14, 18, 22, 26, 34, 41
PENDERGRASS     3, 6, 10, 28, 34
PETERS         67
PEW             3
PHELPS         12, 24, 25, 26, 27, 30, 68, 88
PHILIPS        56
PIKE            6, 17, 25, 38, 42, 52, 55, 56, 82
PITTS          70, 93
POINER          1, 19
POLARD         18
POLLARD        31, 50, 56, 57, 60, 79, 84, 86, 97
POPE            2, 22, 28, 34, 39, 56, 60, 67, 72, 73, 74, 79, 82,
               83, 85, 88, 97
POTER          50
POTTER         51, 67
PRATER         12, 64
PRATOR         32, 56
PRAYTOR        18
PRESLEY        46, 49, 95
PRESTLEY        2


QUALLS         47, 68
QUALS          47
QUARLES        42


RAINS          17, 68
RANDOLPH       19
RANKIN         13, 22, 23, 24, 25, 26, 27, 30, 32, 33, 35, 36, 37,
               43, 44, 45, 46, 48, 50, 52, 53, 54, 56, 57, 58, 59,
               60, 61, 65, 67, 68, 69, 73, 75, 80, 81, 84, 86, 87,
               88, 91, 93, 94, 95
RAWLINGS        6, 29, 64
READ           15, 88
```

```
REAL            1, 30, 97
REAVELY         47
REAVESS         23
REAVICE         15, 89
REAVIS          28, 71, 74
REAVISS         56, 58, 67
RECTOR          18, 40, 44, 46, 49, 55, 65, 76, 78, 91
REDWINE          4, 5, 7, 12, 37, 56
REED             3, 48, 55, 60, 61, 65
REEL            37, 52
REID             6, 65
REINS           73, 77
RENFRO           5, 8, 28, 31, 51, 55, 84, 88
RENFROE         15, 93
RENFROW         92
REVICE           5, 6, 8, 12, 70, 72
REVIS            5, 92
RIGHT           39, 40, 66, 67, 73
RIGSBY          81
RILEY           16
ROBERSON         1, 4, 5, 7, 9, 10, 11, 12, 13, 14, 15, 17, 18, 19,
                22, 25, 26, 27, 28, 29, 30, 31, 32, 33, 34, 37, 39,
                40, 41, 43, 44, 45, 46, 47, 50, 51, 52, 56, 57, 61,
                63, 65, 66, 68, 69, 70, 72, 74, 79, 85, 88, 89, 92,
                93, 97
RODGER           1
RODGERS         74
ROGERS           4, 5, 10, 14, 16, 21, 22, 23, 35, 39, 41, 44, 45,
                51, 53, 55, 64, 82, 92
ROLLINGS        67
ROMINES         89
ROSE            23
RUDD            50, 51
RUSH            31, 73, 88, 94, 97
RUSSEL          97
RUSSELL         17


SALES           18
SCARBORRY       81
SCHOOLFIELD      1, 3, 4, 5, 6, 7, 8, 9, 10, 11, 12, 13, 14, 18,
                20, 21, 22, 31, 33, 34, 36, 40, 41, 44, 49, 61, 76,
                78, 85, 86, 88, 89, 91, 97
SCISSOM         18
SCOTT           92
SEAG             3
SEAGRAVES       60, 72, 97
SEARBERRY       60
SEGRAVES        38
SELBY           25, 31, 67, 93
SHEAREL         94
SHEARL          92
SHEARLET        96
SHEILDS         49
```

```
SHELBY          37
SHELTON         63
SHERELL         12
SHERIL          33, 92
SHERILL          5,  8,  10,  14,  19,  25,  27,  28,  51,  56,  60,  62,  71,
                86,  88,  93,  94,  07
SHERILLS         8
SHERLEY          6,  84,  98
SHERLY          31,  65
SHERRIL         33
SHERRILL        15,  72,  77,  91,  97
SHIRLEY         49
SIMMONS          9,  18,  45,  64,  82
SKILERN         94
SKILES          64,  74
SKILLERN         5,  6,  13,  29,  30,  34,  42,  50,  56,  58,  90,  92,  94,
                96,  97
SLOAN           76,  89
SLONN           82
SLOWN           15
SMITH            2,  3,  4,  5,  6,  7,  8,  14,  16,  17,  18,  20,  27,  28,
                30,  31,  36,  40,  41,  42,  43,  44,  45,  47,  48,  49,  50,
                51,  52,  54,  60,  62,  63,  64,  65,  68,  69,  70,  71,  73,
                74,  76,  79,  80,  84,  86,  87,  90,  93,  97,  98
SNODGRASS       84
SNOTGRASS        3
SPARKMAN         2
SPARKS           1,  18,  34
SPEARS          58,  67,  68,  89
SPRING           3,  11,  22,  27,  32,  39,  42,  52,  57,  58,  76,  88,  91
SPRINGS         22,  32
STANDEFER       13,  60,  73,  86,  88
STANDEPHER      86
STANDIFER        9
STEP            16
STEPHENS         1,  2,  4,  6,  22,  25,  26,  31,  38,  40,  46,  49,  52,
                58,  60,  62,  65,  66,  69,  70,  73,  75,  76,  80,  83,  84,
                85,  86,  88,  89,  90,  91,  94,  95,  96,  97,  98
STEVENS         42
STONE            8,  64,  67
STORY            7
STRANAHAN       10,  32,  44,  57,  64,  74,  75,  91
STRICKLIN       64
STUBS           41,  44,  56,  59,  60,  64
SULLIVAN        64,  76
SUTHERLAND      58,  88,  95
SUTTON          20,  64
SWAFFORD         2,  5,  12,  17,  18,  21,  31,  32,  41,  42,  43,  49,  56,
                57,  58,  59,  64,  65,  67,  69,  74,  75,  76,  77,  79,  84,
                85,  88,  90,  92,  94,  96,  97
SWANER          63
```

```
TAUER            31
TEATERS           2, 93
TEETERS          21
TERRY            18, 23, 32, 53
TETARS           93
TETERS           24, 36, 58, 67, 79, 82
THOMAS            1, 3, 4, 5, 6, 7, 9, 13, 14, 15, 17, 18, 21, 22,
                 23, 24, 25, 28, 29, 31, 32, 34, 35, 37, 39, 40, 41,
                 42, 43, 44, 45, 46, 47,48, 49, 50, 52, 53, 55, 56,
                 57, 58, 60, 62, 63, 64, 65, 66, 67, 68, 69, 70, 71,
                 74, 76, 88, 98
THOMPSON          2, 8, 20, 32, 38, 50, 74
THROPSHIRE        6
THURMAN          13, 14, 15, 17, 30, 32, 34, 35, 36, 41, 42, 44, 47,
                 50, 53, 54, 56, 64, 65, 67, 68, 71, 72, 73, 74, 75,
                 76, 77, 78, 79, 80, 81, 86, 87, 91, 95
TOLLET           25
TOLLETT           2, 8, 9, 10, 11, 18, 22, 37, 38, 46, 58, 60, 62,
                 71, 76, 78, 88, 89
TOMPSON          95
TUCKER           62, 74
TULLOSS           1, 2, 4, 5, 6, 7, 9, 10, 11, 12, 13, 18, 19, 23,
                 24, 39, 41, 51, 57, 59, 61, 66, 67, 71, 73, 76, 77,
                 80, 81, 82, 83, 85, 86, 87, 88, 89, 92, 94
TURNER            3, 97


VANDAVER         46
VERNON            9, 11, 13, 14, 22, 25, 30, 31, 32, 34, 38, 40, 42,
                 52, 56, 60, 68, 74, 79, 88, 94
VICONY           64


WAIT             33
WALKER            2, 4, 5, 6, 7, 8, 9, 10, 13, 18, 19, 21, 22, 23,
                 28, 33, 34, 35, 38, 39, 40, 42, 46, 49, 51, 53, 54,
                 56, 57, 59, 65, 66, 69, 70, 71, 73, 74, 75, 76, 81,
                 85, 86, 87, 89, 91, 92, 93, 97
WALLS            10
WELCH            82, 90
WHEELER           4, 5, 10, 11, 12, 13, 14, 22, 23, 24, 25, 26,
                 39, 44, 45, 51, 52, 56, 57, 60, 73, 77
WHITE            40, 41, 50, 51, 56, 60, 68, 79, 94
WHITESIDE         6, 13, 14, 15, 17, 18, 22, 24, 25, 26, 27, 28, 30,
                 31, 32, 34, 35, 36, 37, 39, 40, 41, 42, 43, 44, 45,
                 46, 48, 50, 51, 52, 53, 54, 56, 57, 58, 59, 60, 61,
                 65, 68, 69, 70, 73, 74, 75, 77, 78, 79, 80, 83, 84,
                 86, 87, 90, 91, 94, 96, 97
WHITTENBURG      14, 18, 61
WIATT            46
WILCOX            4, 11, 64
WILLCOX           1
WILLIAMSON       97
WILLOUGHBY       91
```

WILLSON	3
WILOUGHBY	43
WILSON	25, 50
WILTT	33
WOODS	40, 49, 97
WOOTON	21
WORLEY	3
WORTHING	14
WORTHINGTON	3, 5, 13, 17, 22, 28, 29, 40, 41,42, 44, 45, 46, 48, 56, 60, 62, 68, 73, 75, 81, 88, 96
WRIGHT	2, 18, 34, 38
WRITT	89
WYATT	42
YORK	46
YOUNG	55